If I Can Smile, I Can Live

LISA BRODEUR

IF I CAN SMILE, I CAN LIVE
Copyright © 2023 **Lisa Brodeur.**

No part of this publication may be reproduced, distributed, or transmitted in any form or by any means, including photocopying, recording, or other electronic or mechanical methods, without the prior written permission of the publisher, except in the case of brief quotations embodied in reviews and certain other non-commercial uses permitted by copyright law.

Authorunit
17130 Van Buren Blvd., Ste. 238,
Riverside, CA 92504
877-826-5888
www.authorunit.com

Because of the dynamic nature of the Internet, any web addresses or links contained in this book may have changed since publication and may no longer be valid. The views expressed in the work are solely those of the author and do not necessarily reflect the views of the publisher, and the publisher hereby disclaims any responsibility for them.

Any people depicted in stock imagery provided by Getty images are models, and such images are being used for illustrative purposes only.

ISBN 979-8-89030-258-8 (Paperback)
ISBN 979-8-89030-108-6 (Ebook)

Printed in the United States of America

Contents

Acknowledgment ix
Dedication x
Chapter One 1
Chapter Two 4
Chapter Three 12
Chapter Four 18
Chapter Five 22
Chapter Six 24
Chapter Seven 35
Chapter Eight 42
Chapter Nine 49
Chapter Ten 56
Chapter Eleven 61
Chapter Twelve 64
Chapter Thirteen 70
Chapter Fourteen 76
Chapter Fifteen 83
Chapter Sixteen 94
Chapter Seventeen 99
Chapter Eighteen 105
Chapter Nineteen 119
Chapter Twenty 130
Last Chapter 141

Acknowledgment

$\mathcal{I}$ hope you will find my book to be an inspiration to you, to never give up no matter what your challenge is in life. I hope you will look at your dream and follow it through the best you can. Remember, a disability is what you make of it, find the ability in you, and make it happen.

Let my story inspire you to make changes within yourself. Do not drive impaired in any form. Appreciate your body and everything you can do; you really don't realize what you have until it is taken from you!

Life is short, live it the best you can! BE UNSTOPPABLE!

Dedication

This book is dedicated to my parents Michael and Lisa Brodeur. I have been blessed with parents that really care about me and showed me unconditional love. From the time I was born my mother has been by my side giving me all the love a mom can give and beyond. Thank you for always being by my side for the good and bad. You have showed me strength, courage, determination, and to never give up no matter what life has thrown me. Thank you for being you, I love you Mom.

My father Michael gave me his unconditional love at the young age of one in a half years old. There was nothing he wouldn't do for me, he truly loved me as his own child. He showed me a father's love and made me feel wanted and accepted for who I was. Thank you for giving me your love and for adopting me. I am so proud to be your son and to carry your name with me always. You were taken from me way too soon, but someday we will meet again. I love you Dad, R.I.P.

This book is dedicated to my stepfather Lenny, my sisters, and Michael DiDonato. Thank you all for always being there for me with your love, support, and your time. You all had helped, in making my dreams come true, and to be the person I am today. Thank you for letting me live life to the fullest and finding ways to make me smile! I am blessed with you all in my life. Thank you.

This book is dedicated to my doctors that have operated on me and took chances where other doctors denied me medical attention.

There are just no words to say how thankful I am to have had Dr. Gerald McGillicuddy and his team who saved my life the night of our crash on 11/1/1997, and on 10/28/2022. Both surgeries were challenging and life threatening and you stepped up both times without hesitation. You knew I was a fighter, and giving up was not an option for me. Thank you for giving me another chance at life where others just didn't care.

Dr. Michael Glotzbecker, and his team stepped up after many doctors refused to operate on me, the surgery was just too complicated and serious. You took the chance because you knew I was strong, and I had the will to live.

Without these surgeries I wouldn't be here today. Its doctors like both of you, that truly make a difference in so many lives. Thank you both for taking the chance on me.

This book is dedicated to all the prayer warriors that keep me in their thoughts and prayers especially when I am hospitalized.

I do believe in the power of prayer, thank you!

Chapter One

I often wondered is this real. Is this my life?

Why so much pain?

Why are my bones twisting and turning?

Why can't I move my limbs?

I have so many whys, and now trying to figure out, how do I live a life with all these changes.

It was a quick second, that my ten-year-old life was shattered. How can a ten-year-old life be shattered when I really didn't even start living yet?

All I wanted was my rollerblades that my parents bought me that cold rainy night on November 1st, 1997. I couldn't wait to try them on, and rollerblade in my yard. I was the happiest little boy, it felt like Christmas morning.

My father took me to get some autographs from some hockey players that were at the mall that night. My dad said we would frame the autographs and find a spot on my bedroom wall.

Well, that never happened, instead my father was killed instantly on impact by an impaired driver that was intoxicated and on cocaine. I was in a body that I no longer known, fighting for every breath I took.

I don't remember the first several months or Christmas of 1997. I was told I was in a comatose state. Machines were breathing for me, keeping me alive.

Months later opening my eyes realizing I am in a rehab hospital. I can hear but I can't respond. My mother is with me with some women that I have never seen before.

They are talking about me! I was sweating, having spasms, I can't move or talk?

What is going on?

I had so many questions all inside of me wondering, what is happening?

Where is my father, my two little sisters?

Why is my mom injured, what happened to her arm?

Where are my rollerblades that I bought at the mall before our crash?

All I knew that life was different; nurses were trying to make me comfortable, repositioning me in bed. My right arm was in a cast. I had different people giving me bed baths.

I have a catheter in! What is this?

Looking to my mom for answers, but I can't speak!

I was trapped, trapped in a body that I don't know!

Is this permanent? Is this a dream?

My mom explaining to me that we were in a car crash, and my sisters are home recovering. Your daddy was seriously injured, he passed away. I am still healing from my injuries. You were badly injured and have a traumatic brain injury and every day you our getting stronger and you need to keep fighting. We are at Spaulding Rehab in Boston, MA trying to heal and get better.

My progress was slow, mom always by my side day and night helping me with eating, therapy, and memories of my life.

Finally, I am going home after eleven months of being hospitalized, so many surgeries and therapies I had.

Home is different, furniture was moved around and now a hospital bed is where my couch was.

My aunt Jean is helping my mom to take care of me, while my little sisters are running around.

Why can't I run and play with them?

I don't want to be in this bed, I want my own bed upstairs, I have a bedroom.

Why can't I sleep in my own room?

My body is in so much pain, I am crying,

If I Can Smile, I Can Live

"HELP ME PLEASE," mom tries to help me, but she can't stop the spasms.

I want my father; I want my old body back.

I still didn't even try out my rollerblades.

I had so many changes, adjustments, and questions, that needed answers, that this can't be real!

It must be a dream, but why am I not waking up from it?

This nightmare wouldn't go away. Someone please WAKE me up, and take my PAIN away!

Chapter Two

It took me a year before I really started to understand what happened to me. I was only Ten years old when I was hit by a drunk driver and someone that was on cocaine.

When I came out of my comatose state, I was always in severe pain, screaming from having severe spasms. I realized I could cry out, but I also noticed I no longer had any tears! I looked at my mom to HELP me, but she couldn't, her tears would flow down her face. I would keep getting repositioned in bed by the nurses or put in my wheelchair, but it didn't work. Sometimes it made my spasms worse.

My mom would massage my legs trying to wean out the spasm, but it did nothing. My pain was just so severe all I could do was sweat and scream out loud. My mother was helpless just like me. I had medicine but the meds wouldn't even touch my pain!

In my eleven-year-old body, I wanted to get out of bed, go run, play all my sports like I use to.

I was trying to understand why couldn't I get up, move my arms and legs?

Why can't I talk?

Why am I struggling with eating?

Why am I in diapers? I can't even brush my teeth.

What happened to me???

I had so many questions and just couldn't understand. I would look at my mom in fear not realizing that this was permanent for me.

My mother knew I needed answers, she told me about our crash, and what happened to me. She always reminded me; I was still healing and each day I would hopefully improve. In some ways I did improve, but in other ways it just got worse.

I not only lost my life and what I knew, I also lost my father, my hero. My father, was killed instantly, he never had a chance. I had to accept my father was no longer there and he couldn't be by my side any longer. I was angry; I needed him more than anything.

Why, Why did he die?

Why am I still here suffering?

I wanted to be with my father and be pain free.

My body would no longer work; I am paralyzed, and the pain would not get better.

Why was I left here in this world to suffer?

My life now is in a wheelchair. It was a lot to accept and to have the strength to not give up. My mother wouldn't let me give up, there were so many times I just didn't care and I didn't want to do anything but she made me get up, out of bed, no matter what I said.

Getting out of bed was the best thing to do, it felt good to be dressed and in a different position and going outside.

There were times I couldn't handle being up, I could be at a restaurant or movie theater, and we had to leave. I would be sweating so badly, we could never be to far from home.

My two little sisters', Kimberly and Katie always handled it very well, they understood I was in pain and didn't cry to stay. I was lucky they were so understanding for their age.

My sisters were only four and six years old and now they were helping me, I was no longer taking care of them. What a role reverse. They would try so hard to help me and make me laugh. I couldn't even smile, because of the two strokes I had. These two little angels were my best friends; they kept life for me interesting. They helped me come out of my comatose state. They taught me what they new, singing barney and nursery rhymes and singing the ABC's. They would spend lots of time with me in my bed, consoling me, giving me cold wet towels to help me from sweating. My mother taught my sister's how to move my legs to try to help with my spasms. Their little hands would rub my legs and what a blessing it was to me.

Even though I was so injured, I still needed to attend a school program. My mother found me a great school in Canton, MA called the Mass Hospital School. This school was a distance from my hometown in Southbridge so I would leave on a Sunday and come home on Friday nights.

This school had other challenging students, some in wheelchairs, others walking. I had to leave my friends that I once knew, and had to adjust to all new people. It was extremely difficult trying to make friends while I was so injured. I could no longer talk, bathe, feed or do anything for myself, it was strangers helping me now, people that I learned to adapt to.

It was a huge adjustment for me, I had behaviors and pain that I never knew existed. I had so much impulsivity, that I would put my fingers in my mouth pulling at my lip/cheek, giving me habits I never had.

I just wanted to speak and ask to be repositioned or have a drink. I had to wait patiently for someone to take the time and figure out what I needed. At times I would wait a while for a staff member to come in my room, I was having spasms, and I needed more medicine. Eventually an attendant would come in, they would see me sweating badly, in pain, soaked though all my sheets. My CNA would grab me a cold towel to try to help cool me down, it felt good, I loved it. I would eventually get meds, but they barely touched me.

At times I wished I would have died; the pain was so unbearable. If I was lucky, the medicine would make me sleepy, and I would finally get some sleep.

I was consistently placed in cast, trying to help my severe dystonia. My right arm was so tight, that I was put in a cast. The cast worked for my right arm but now my muscle tone is in my left arm. The doctor decided to put a cast on my left arm, but I couldn't tolerate it. My blood pressure was always high, and I couldn't bear the pain. We had to remove the cast.

Casting was placed on both my legs, since my severe dystonia curved both my feet. Casting didn't work so I had surgery. I had to wear foot braces for years until my muscle tone won once again. My tone curved my right foot and now I can no longer wear a shoe. Thankfully my left foot is okay to be able to wear a shoe.

If I Can Smile, I Can Live

I was trying to understand why this is happening?

All I wanted was to try to stand again. Perhaps my brain could heal and in time I could walk again.

I cried often out loud; my pain was unbearable to handle. The spasms would not stop.

The Dystonia now traveled through my whole body. It took my left arm, both my feet and now in my right kneecap and rotated my right hip. I was put in a full SPICA body cast for three months after my hip surgery. That was hell; I was bedridden, I would sweat, and at times, itchy, and there was no way of itching my body through the cast.

I had to be bathed and toileted, and when I got C-Diff it was even harder to keep my casting clean. It was very difficult for my mother, but somehow, she did it!

I had to wear a Body jacket most of the day for many years since my muscle tone was in my spine. In the beginning I was horrible, I fought my mother so bad that she had a really hard time to put my jacket on. I would have to wear a tight t-shirt that could not wrinkle and put gold Bond powder under my armpits since this would toughen up my skin.

My muscle tone always made me lean to the right side, so my Body jacket would always dig under my armpits. I would curse the jacket because it bothered me so badly. I just wanted to get it off of me, I would sweat, I was angry that I had to wear such a tight jacket all the time.

This hard, tight contraption that made me sweat was suppose to help keep my spine from curving, but my muscle tone was so severe, that it didn't work. We were trying to prevent surgery from happening.

I wore the body jacket for twelve-hour days, and some years even when I was sleeping. I only had a break in the morning and at night when bathing. Sad to say the jacket didn't hold me, severe dystonia took my spine and curved it so badly that I had no choice but to have a spinal fusion surgery.

After years of having a body jacket, I got so use to having one on, that when I had my spinal fusion surgery, I didn't want to give up my jacket. It was part of me; it was all I knew. After a few days I adjusted to not having it on and never wanted it ever again.

It's been many years since my spinal fusion surgery back in 2003. I am loosing my neck now due to severe dystonia, and since the hardware let go in my back, it is not serving its purpose any longer. Now I have an infection in my spine and hardware. This is serious; I have major medical decisions to make. My mom took me to a doctor and he suggested that we do a clean out but the surgery could only happen if he could form a team of doctors.

I am looking to have three to five surgeries within two weeks time, to do a cleanout of my infection. If one organism is left in my back the infection could all come back.

If I choose not to do this and my infection turns to a staff infection or other type of infection, I am told I might not survive the surgery. My bones and tissue are growing over the hardware and that makes this surgery much more difficult.

This surgery is major. I am stuck, I don't want to die, I am too young.

I have been through a lot in my short life and suffer a lot, but guess what? I love my family and I found ways to make me happy. I am not ready to give up!! I have had Twenty-five surgeries. I am only 28 years old. I have had brain, feet, intestinal, hip, spinal Fusion, baclophen pump's, twisted testical, shunt's, and a filter screen for a blood clot put in. I have dealt with a few infections that required surgeries. It's been never easy for me.

I can honestly say, I have had enough! I am sick of hospitals, except for the pretty nurses. I just want to live my life the best that I can and be happy. I would give anything to have my old body back. I miss running and being active and doing all the simple things we all take for granted. I do realize that this could never happen but it doesn't mean I don't wish or want it.

Always remember life is 10% of what is given to us, and 90% of what we make of it. My 10% is the hell I go through medically! The 90% is my attitude and having my family and friends.

I try to live life and make happy memories. I love to play pranks on my family and friends, whether it's scaring them with a spider or when they are sleeping and pour water on them. Or better yet lock my PCA's in my closet! I always try to find fun, luckily I have a silly and fun household, we are not serious people, and sadly we are use of things going wrong that we try not to dwell on all the bad news medically.

If I Can Smile, I Can Live

My mom and I have been to many doctors, and we have been turned down numerous times for the removal of my hardware in my spine. The doctor that wanted to do the clean out, could not form a team of doctors, so now I am back to square one again. We are sitting ducks waiting for my infection to turn. I have gone three years so far, I am hoping I will go many more years. My mother will continue to search for a doctor for me because she will never give up, and hopefully soon we will find one.

One doctor described me in a canoe without a paddle! Imagine that! No Paddle! Thank god the canoe won't sink, I am not ready to give up on life! I still have lots to do here on earth!

Michael and Lisa 1994

Kyle 9 years old, with his sister's Kimberly and Katie, 1996

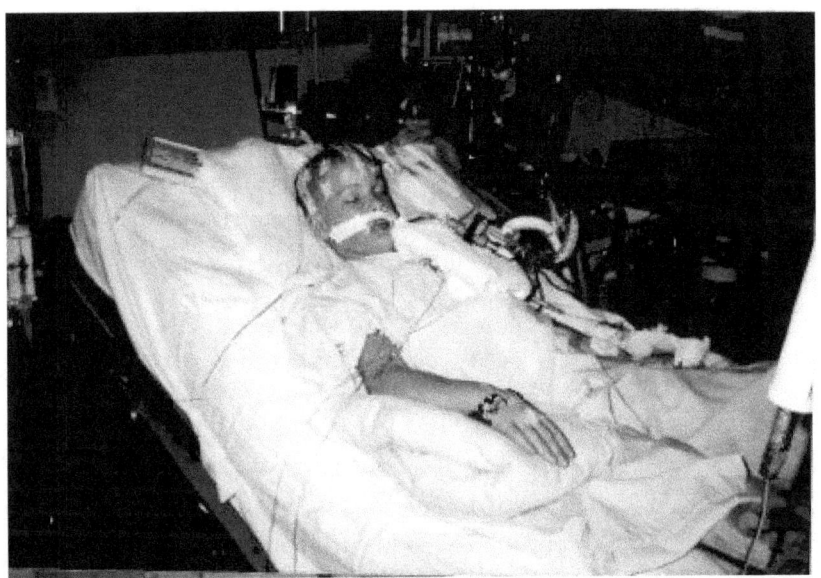

Kyle, 10 years old, in a coma and on a ventilator for 7 weeks

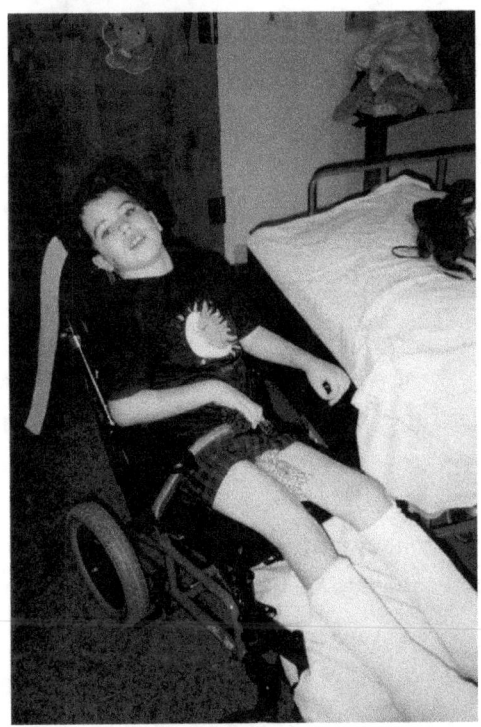

Kyle in a conscious state after six months, 1998

Chapter Three

My first year of life was full of love from both my parents, I reached all my milestones of sitting up, rolling over and walking by nine months of age. My parents had their hands full with me. I was a handsome little baby with brunette/blond curls and a very chubby and happy little boy. I loved to eat, play and be with my cousins and family. I slept through the night in my crib, holding my special blanket. I loved my parents.

I had my first birthday at my aunty Patty's house; I had many family members, and cousins that attended. I received lots of presents. It was a great first birthday.

Later that night, my parents were fighting, and things got messy, my mother said. It got so bad that my father was forced to leave our home. From then on, she never went back to him and raised me herself.

I was so young, I just turned one.

My father only came to pick me up once in a while, it was never consistent. The first couple years I would wait by the window waiting for my father truck to pull up, sometimes he did, other times he didn't. I would end up crying, not understanding why he told me he was coming and then not show up. It was hard, I was so young, I didn't understand.

My life with mom went on, mom now worked full time. Life was hard financially, she didn't get much child support and at times it wasn't paid at all.

Luckily, I always had what I needed, and never went without.

During the nice weather we went to a lot of parks so I could play, and I hung out at my aunties houses and played with my cousins often.

If I Can Smile, I Can Live

Once a week mom and I would walk up town to eat at a pizza shop. Life was simple but, I was loved by my mother.

Mom worked two jobs to try to make ends meat.

Her first job was at United Lens Company in Southbridge, she worked in an office from eight to five. Her second job was one weekend night, either a Friday, Saturday or Sunday; she worked for a caterer company. My auntie Laurie babysat me mostly or my mom worked late at night and she would pay a sitter. I have to say my mother worked hard to support our needs.

When I was one in a half mom started dating a man she met at work, Michael Brodeur, she said I loved Mike from the minute I met him. My first time meeting him I was told we played on the floor, I jumped on his back and I was given a horse ride, we had so much fun. Meeting Mike was life changing for my mom and I; he treated us good and was always there for both of us.

After a year or so of Mike and my mom dating I asked Mike if I could call him daddy" mom said I was sitting on him and I just came out with it. I was around two in half then.

Mike went to my mother and asked her how he should respond to me?

Mom said, "We both knew we loved each other, and we figured we would be married in time, so mom said she didn't mind as long as he didn't".

Mike said "He was happy to be called daddy or whatever I wanted",

"He loved me like his own".

Mom said, "I was so happy", from that moment on I called him daddy.

I wanted and needed a father figure so badly and Mike was it for me. Our life changed for the good, and mom and I couldn't of been happier.

Throughout my years till the age of seven years old, I was always wondering will my Biological father really show up and take me out today? Most of the time he never showed, even though we talked and he said he was coming. I was left crying running to my room not understanding why he never showed up.

I had so many questions?

Why would my father hurt me like this?

Why wouldn't he want to come see me?

Did I do something wrong?

Doesn't he even love me?

I guess looking back at it today, my biological father couldn't have loved me, and I can't make him, but I will never understand why he didn't want to be part of my life. I was innocent and a good little boy.

As time went by, it was many months at a time without seeing my biological father, then even to once or twice a year. It was rough on me, as I got older.

When mom and dad became married, mom took daddy's last name. I was almost five years old, and I was thankful that daddy was my family now.

A few months later we found out mom was pregnant. We were all so excited.

Mom asked my father if he wanted a boy or girl and he said,

"He didn't care, he already has a son", and I have to say that made me smile, my father loved me unconditionally.

I was blessed with my little sister Kimberly, then twenty months later, another sister Katie was born. I loved them, and I was the best brother they could have.

But guess what? Everyone in my house had the Brodeur name. I felt left out; I felt a sense of being different and not belonging so I asked my mother if I could have daddy's last name? To me my father was Mike, and I wanted to be a Brodeur, and be like everyone else in my house.

My mom said "Let me talk to dad about it", mom went to dad and told him what just happened. Dad new already because of some of the remarks I said.

My father said, "He didn't care if I added his last name to mine or how we did it, he just wanted me to feel loved and wanted".

Mom, called up my biological father and asked him "If we could do a name change, or add Brodeur to Kyle's name"?

My Biological father said "No".

Mom came to tell me the bad news, I was crying I didn't want to be a Tremblay any longer. Mom just hugged me and had tears and tucked me in telling me how much dad and her loved me.

Mom went downstairs and my father had another idea, he said "What if I adopt Kyle, then legally he will be mine, then we would never have to worry about losing each other".

Mom loved the idea, but will my biological father agree to it? Mom hugged my father, and said 'thank you' and telling him she loved him.

Mom called my biological father up and told him our idea of adoption. She told him he would lose all rights to me, and he wouldn't have to pay child support any longer.

My father said, "He would let Mike adopt me".

Mom was so happy, she was crying. Daddy and mom came to my bedroom and told me the good news. I hugged my father so tight and said, "I can't wait to be a Brodeur".

The next morning my father called an attorney, and we made an appointment to start the paperwork.

When I was nine years old the adoption went through, and I changed my middle name to David because that is my dad's middle name.

My official name now is Kyle David Brodeur, and Michael David Brodeur is my father! I can't be happier!

I will never understand why till this day he doesn't want to be in my life. I do have a brother and sister from my biological father, unfortunately I have never met my brother.

My sister, however, has been in my life since she was born, her name is Breanna. I do hope on meeting my brother someday and I am not sure if he even knows about us.

My mom and Breanna's mother, Cheryl are friends and they come over frequently. I am very close to Breanna, and I love her, she's the baby sister. Unfortunately her father isn't in her life either. We both don't understand why and how he can have two children and be so absent from our lives.

We both look forward to the day when we can meet our brother. Hopefully it will be sooner than later.

My parents have given me a great life, we did so many things together, and I had all the love I needed, I had a real family.

I played so many sports and was involved in lots of activities. I was a busy little guy. I can honestly say I had a great ten years besides the hardship of not seeing my biological father.

My father was so happy for me, to have his name, thinking if something ever happened to mom I was his, he wouldn't have to worry about fighting for me. Who would of thought, my father would get killed by an impaired driver later that year and myself fighting for every breath to stay alive.

It was a crash that should of never happened! You just don't know what life is going to throw you.

After a full year I came out of my comatose state I had to relearn how to live again, it was extremely hard and so many challenges especially now being paralyzed and dependent on every need.

A new addition was built to my old house so it would be accessible for me. This is where my mom met Lenny he was the electrician, and they later married in the year, 2000. I love Lenny, he was good to my sisters and myself.

We built a new home in the year 2001, and it's all-accessible for me. I have everything I need; I have lived here now for Twenty-three years. I hope to never have to move.

As the years went on, life was extremely hard, so many hospital stays, surgeries, and struggles for mom and me. My two little sisters Kimberly and Katie had their own struggles still trying to accept daddy is no longer here and healing from within.

As a family there was so much to handle with me, I was always in so much pain. I couldn't play with my sisters and pick them up and hold them like I use to. Life was surely different. It was very hard, I had to adjust to everyone taking care of me now and not being able to do anything for myself.

Lenny had his own issues going on and my mom and Lenny got divorced after six years of marriage. This was extremely hard for all of us because we loved Lenny, but mom didn't have a choice, she had to divorce a man she loved.

Once again, we had a lot of adjusting to do, life was surely different. My sister's are all getting older now, graduating high school, going to college, graduating college, and now finding their partner for life. My baby sister, Breanna, is attending college and she will graduate in one more year.

If I Can Smile, I Can Live

After seven years of my mom and Lenny being divorced, I am happy to say they are back together. They gave their relationship another try and it's going great. They are both so happy and they never stopped loving each other.

Lenny is a great stepfather and I know he will always be there for my sisters and I. If it wasn't for him I wouldn't of been able to do some of the activities I have done. Lenny really stepped up to help my mom discover ways to make all the things I wanted to try happen. I can honestly say, I have lived life to my fullest so far.

One thing I love about my family is that even though I may be paralyzed and so limited to what I can do, they never say no to any adventure I would like to try. My family always finds ways for me to do everything, they let me live and experience life the best I can. I do take a lot of risk, but if I didn't, I wouldn't have the many experiences that I have had. I would just be sitting in a wheelchair at such a young age with no experiences and always wondering what it felt like. It isn't fun just watching everyone else. Now I can say I did that and what I thought about it.

I have experienced Kali River Rapids, jet ski's, bee gun shooting, Tower of Terror, waterslides, rollercoasters, regular rides, swimming under the water, swimming with the dolphins, swimming with the stingrays and baby sharks, jumping off the diving board, travelling, flying, parasailing and boats. I am very fortunate and thankful that my family helps me have these experiences. Always remember if you WANT it bad enough, make it HAPPEN!!

Chapter Four

I am having no luck finding a doctor. I have been denied thirteen times because of the severity of the infection in my spine, I am so frustrated. I am forming sinuses in my back that leaves holes so the infection is now leaking out. I currently have three holes that leak continuously. My blood test results show a severe infection, but it didn't go to my blood stream yet and I am not having any fevers. My mom was told that I am falling in a one percent category and their isn't much we can do. We have to wait for me to spike a fever and then we need to find out what kind of infection it is. Can it be treated with an antibiotic, or will it be life threatening to me?

I need to remove all my hardware in my back, and most likely my baclofen pump is infected also. If I did have surgery my pump could also get disconnected which controls all my pain for my spasms. This would be very painful if I loose the pump. My spasms and pain would become unbearable!

Why does this surgery have to be so huge and complicated? It's hard to find a doctor that wants to get involved at this point. My orthopedic doctor retired, and he only took extreme cases like me, he even tried to find me a doctor but he had no luck. My mom and I have been all over Boston trying to find a doctor, they all seem to say NO!

One day leaving a doctor's office with my mom, I grabbed her wrist and was squeezing it. I was trying to take in everything the doctor said. I realized the surgery was so complex and doctors didn't want to be involved. What do I Do? I was scared!!!

Mom had to tell me to stop squeezing her, I was hurting her.

I looked at her and said, "I don't want to die".

If I Can Smile, I Can Live

Her eyes filled up in tears, and she said, "Don't worry, you have always been different, and we made it this long, I am sure we will find a doctor, and everything will be okay". "We will keep searching and take one day at a time". We went to our car to go home once again with no answers.

Later that night when she was putting me to bed, I told her I have been thinking and I wanted to start my bucket list, just in case anything happened to me.

She said, "Bucket list, what's on this bucket list?"

I told her I wanted to write my own book on my feelings on what I have been through. She thought it was a great idea, and here we are doing it now. I am hoping my book will help people that are unfortunate like me to help them live life to the fullest and not ever give up no matter what.

I want all caregivers to understand what it is like for us when we can't communicate or have to wait for every need in life.

What it's like going from a normal and healthy child to an adult and being dependent on every need.

Even though life is hard we have to remember if We Can Smile, We Can Live! We just have to be extra creative and have the support system around us to let us live life to the fullest.

My second thing on my bucket list is driving. I want to drive a car.

She said, "How am I going to do that"?

My third is running through Disney with my teammate Mike.

Mom said, "Where did you ever come up with that?

She never heard of it. She promised we would look into it, and then ask Mike if he is willing to go to Disney and run this race with you.

Mike DiDonato is like a brother to me, mom met Mike in a bike shop in 2011. They started talking about how I became paralyzed, and Mike felt bad for me since I was so athletic before our crash, and now wheelchair bound. Mike offered to make me a running chair and possibly run a race or two together. That one or two races turned into many races together and we our Unstoppable, we make a great team.

" Anything else" she said, yes I want to go to Mississippi on a riverboat cruise.

Mom laughed and said, "Boy, I have a lot to look into. Your bucket list is not easy and very expensive.

I just put my thumbs up for agreeing with her and now I will watch her make it all happen. I have to say she hates telling me no, and I know she always tries hard so if there is a way she will find it for me.

Later that day we talked about my book that I wanted to write. Mom started asking me lots of questions and I would answer them, and she took notes. Then she takes my answers and writes accordingly. After she is done writing a Chapter she reads it to me then I make changes to it. I have to say I love doing this; I look forward to the questions and answering them. I know this book will be time consuming, but I really want to share my thoughts and feelings and have my own book.

At night, I pulled up the Disney race for her to see on YouTube, she was amazed and thought it would be so much fun to do. She called up Mike, my running partner and asked him if he would be willing to go to Disney and run a race? He talked to his wife and she didn't mind if he went so he said "Yes, let's do it". Now the question was how do we get accepted? Will Run Disney let a duo like us let me be pushed in a running chair by someone else in their Disney Princess race? I decided to write a letter to Disney asking them for permission and now we sit and wait for an answer.

Later in the week mom looked up the Mississippi River Cruise, it sounded like a great trip. She told me she wasn't sure she could pull that one off because of the expense of it. Mom offered that she could take me there and take a cruise on the river and just do things a little different. I said, "No, I want the river cruise."

A few months later my mom and I were doing a book event at CMSC Driving School in West Boylston. We go to the driving school and talk to the parents of our young driver's and share our story with them on how an impaired driver forever changed our life. My mom takes her book with her, A Mother's Journey Through Faith, Hope, and Courage and if the parents decide they want the book for their child to read or for themselves to bring awareness they can purchase it.

Tim Cooney was present and he was saying how his school even helps individuals with disability's obtain a license. Immediately my hand went up asking if I can obtain a license?

Tim smiled and said, "I don't know about a license but maybe we can get you to drive a vehicle."

I picked my head up and put a big smile on my face. My mom let him know this was on my bucket list to do. She was so happy! I was wondering, could this really happen, and how would I do it?

I left CMSC that night feeling so happy. My bucket list is being worked on and I can't wait to make my wishes come true.

Chapter Five

Can you believe I got to drive a van? Yes, it really did happen, Tim Cooney from CMSC Driving School made it happen.

My mom woke me up in the morning and said we were going to CMSC to speak to the parents about her book. It was a normal thing we did so I didn't think anything of it. We pulled into the school parking lot, and I was taken out of the van. Tim came outside with Don Sampson his driving instructor.

Tim said" Today is the big day I promised you, and you are going to drive a Van".

I had to honestly say I was in shock; I didn't know what to do.

Don pulled up with an accessible Van, opened the side door, he extended the ramp out. Don rolled me in, and before I knew it, I was in front of the steering wheel. Don explained everything to me about the controls, emergency break, and seatbelt. I had a handle on the wheel, that I could move to make turns, but I preferred a lever, that I could control easier. This lever also controlled the gas and brakes. I drove in a parking lot with Don, and I even had passengers. My mom was busy taking picture.

When I was driving, I thought it was exciting. I do realize I could never do this by myself, but Don was there to help me steer, make sure I gave gas and to break when needed. I had a smile on my face the whole time. I know I could never drive on a road, but thanks to Tim and Don I was lucky enough to experience it. I wish it never had to end but at least I can say, I drove a van and I can cross it off my bucket list!

If I Can Smile, I Can Live

My mom heard back from Disney, they are allowing Mike and I to run in the Princess Race in February. We had to register early online, and it was a process, it fills up very fast. Mike and I are excited to be participating in this race. Disney said this is the first time they ever had a duo like Team Unstoppable running one of their races.

Disney gave us some requirements like a bike helmet and light reflectors for my bike. Now I get to go to the bike shop and buy a helmet and I will see what Mike wants to do about the reflectors. We have a lot of planning to do.

I love my new running chair and it evens comes apart for travelling. This will be our first race together out of state, and who would think it would be Disney!

Yes, I am Excited!

Chapter Six

My mother and I are off for another sedation at Children's Hospital in Boston, I go every thirteen weeks. Today I am having my Botox injections, thankfully we are running on time. I will be having a blood test to check on my infection, in my back.

Dr. Nimic asked "How I have been"? Mom tells the story like she does to every doctor. "I can't find a doctor to take Kyle on and expresses concern about my infection and my white cell count, is extremely high".

This time, Dr. Nimic said "She was going to try to help us find a doctor"! "Kyle has come to far, to give up on him now; I will find a doctor to remove his spinal fusion hardware".

We were both so relieved and happy.

The next day my mom receives a phone call from Dr. Nimic, stating my infection level has resin again, and she may have found us a doctor.

The doctor would call us in a few days. The following week we received a phone call from a doctor at Children's stating his concern about my infection and letting us know another doctor is willing to see me.

This doctor was forwarded my current cat scan and reports and said to have me come in. The doctor and mom spoke for a while and he expressed concern on not doing anything, and if we did do something how serious it was.

We are in between a rock and a double hard rock he stated.

After mom's phone call, she came to me and said, "We may finally have a doctor and he wants to see you, after reviewing your medical records".

Mom was in tears; I had my thumbs up in shock.

Mom said, "You will never guess his first name?

"I smiled", because that usually means his name is Michael. This is always a great sign for me since this is my father's name.

We talked about having my hardware removed, and if I didn't, the consequences were not good. The infection would eventually spread to my bloodstream, and there was a high chance of getting meningitis.

We talked a little about it, and I said "Mom F--- it! Let's take it all out, let's do the surgery!"

She thought it was my only chance of surviving this nightmare, but realizing we have a lot ahead of us. We decided to go talk to the doctor at Children's Hospital and see if he has the experience to do this difficult surgery. We wanted to ask what my chances were of even surviving this kind of surgery.

A few days after, we received a call and we set up an appointment to go meet this doctor in two weeks. We were fortunate that the secretary squeezed us in for an appointment.

The day finally came, and we had a snowstorm, there was no way we could go. We all were not happy; we wanted to meet this doctor and hear his thoughts. We scheduled another appointment for the week after, luckily no snow; I was awakened at 5 AM and out of the house for 5:30 AM. Lenny warmed the car up for me, it was near zero degrees.

Off we went to Children's Hospital to meet Dr. Michael Glotzbecker, I was excited but nervous. I listened to the questions and answers Lenny and mom had and it was a lot to take in.

The outcome is, I have a big decision to make, and I am scared to death.

Do I take an antibiotic to help my body fight off anything new that could possibly happen? This med would not help my infection, but it could possibly buy me a little more time to live.

I don't seem to get sick; I only get major problems that need surgery.

The doctor said if I decide to do this difficult surgery, it could possibly take multiple surgeries, if I have complications during the procedure.

If the surgery became too much for my body, the surgeon would have to stop and close me up. I would be put in a comatose state to rest until I would be strong enough to go back to finish the procedure.

I was told I could lose my baclofen pump if my bone is infected, or if the catheter comes out. This is huge, my pump controls my severe spasms. Without this, I am in severe pain, it's a pain like no other, it's unbearable!

I would have to wait months for the infection to clear, before a new one could be placed.

Once the hardware is removed, I could curve more, my spine could be weaker. This is a high possibility, if this were to happen, I would need a new spinal fusion. It is also likely my neck would need to be fixed, since I am losing my ability to keep my head up. So as you can see one surgery leads to many more!

What do I do??

We talked about the procedure, and we all felt the doctor was very confident and young. Being young could be a good thing, especially with staying on your feet for long periods of time and not being shaky with the knife. We decided that Dr. Michael Glotzbecker would be our doctor, if we decide to do this surgery.

We our taking the weekend to discuss it and call the office on Monday with an answer.

It's a very hard decision, I have so many emotions and I am scared. I don't want to die; I am so young. I wonder will there ever be a time in my life that I don't have to have all these major surgeries happen?

Can I ever live life the way I am, paralyzed and be hospital free?

Why more surgeries, isn't twenty-five enough?

How much more will my body take?

How many more chances at life will I have, before I do die?

We all know if I want to continue living, I don't have a choice, I must go ahead with this extremely hard surgery and hope for the best. I know I am strong, and I will give it my all, to survive.

Monday morning came and my mother called to say we are going to do surgery, now we are waiting for a date. In the meantime, we are not going to dwell on this, I have a vacation to get ready for, and soon I will be running through Disney. I am so excited to do this.

I hope my teammate Mike is ready to run his first half marathon and to push me in my new blade he made me. I am happy that Mike is coming to Florida to push me in this race and to help me complete my bucket list. I do realize it is a lot for him to leave his young family for a few days and come to Disney for me.

Mike and I have a special bond, and a great friendship and I am thankful to him for giving me a sport again. Our Team name is "Team Unstoppable" and our quote is "Never Stop Dreaming" the reason being that I have always been Unstoppable no matter what happens to me and I never stopped dreaming of a sport again and thanks to Mike he gave me one.

My Blade, which is my special running chair, is amazing, I am so proud of it. I love going fast and we can even change the tires on this chair to go on rough terrain, or a sandy beach, we call these tires the Fat Blade. This is nice for me, now I can be pushed through the woods in a chair. My motorized chair cannot do this, it is too bumpy. This blade has opened up a new part of life for me and gives me fun and speed. Everyone that is paralyzed or has a disability that prevents them from running, walking or going fast should be lucky enough to have one.

My Blade is amazing and it's all painted. We put the American Flag, New England Patriot's symbol, Team Unstoppable, Never Stop Dreaming on the wheels. Mike even surprised me with putting a picture of my father and my cross that I have tattooed on my arm on a plate in the front. My father is running with me in every race!

Since we our running the princess race I decided to be a prince. I found a costume online, and I have to say I am going to look handsome! I am excited to go, just three more weeks!

The time has come, we have been packing and preparing for our big trip, so much is involved. My mother decided to make a longer vacation for us all, since I haven't been to Florida in a while. We are going to Disney for five nights, then to Daytona Beach for three nights then back to Orlando for four more nights. This should be interesting. My stepfather Lenny will be coming with us, he definitely will be doing a lot of lifting. I am hoping my mom let's me go on the rollercoaster rides. I know she is nervous about that, because of my seizures, so I doubt she will let me.

You wouldn't believe what's involved in taking me away for this amount of time. I will be taking one wheelchair which is a chance we are taking, hoping that it doesn't break on the plane or while we are gone. We are taking another controller just incase it gets damaged while travelling.

I have hospital beds being brought to the different hotels that we are staying at.

We rented a Handicap vehicle to head to Daytona Beach.

I must bring medical supplies, bandages, diapers, protection for the mattress, a wedge for sleeping, medicine and lots of clothes.

I will fill three suitcases myself. The good thing is, after using some of my supplies I have the empty bags to fill up with memories to take home. I'm sure I won't have a problem doing that.

The day has come we are off to Disney! I went through a search at the airport, which was rough on my body. TSA, had Lenny lift me out of my chair, to check my seat cushion on my wheelchair and then take off my sneaker. Thankfully after that was done, we checked on our flight, and we were running on time.

When it was time to board the plane, Lenny carried me to my seat and got me settled. I have to say people our very curious, and you can tell, they probably never seen someone as disabled as me flying.

During the flight I had to sit up straight in my seat, so that was extremely hard for my body. I had a neck travel pillow to keep my neck comfortable, and two small travel pillows for my sides, to help sit up straighter, since I have no trunk support.

I used a small pillow to go in between my legs and a wedge on the floor to rest my leg and foot on.

Throughout the plane ride Lenny kept boosting me up in my chair. Overall, I did great. When it was time to land, I was the last to get off. We had to wait for my wheelchair to be brought to the entrance of the plane. When it arrived, mom put my wheelchair back together again and gathered all my pillows and our personal items then Lenny picked me up and carried me to my wheelchair.

Now off to get our luggage and ride to our Disney hotel. It was a lot, but it was definitely worth it, I am in Florida and ready to have a great time!

Mike and I met in Disney, and we went to get our packets for registration for the Princess race. We were so excited!

Morning came fast, we had to meet at 3 am for the buses. Lenny had to go with Mike to help him with my running chair, they took the wheels off and placed the bike at the bottom of the bus.

Mom and I were waiting for a handicap bus to come, it took a very long time and we ended up late for the race.

When we arrived at Epcot we had to run to where the race begins, my motorized chair can only go so fast. My mom was struggling, she was in pain trying to get me to where Mike was. Lenny came running and took me from mom and brought me to where Mike was. I was immediately put in my running chair.

We had to run with a different set of runners, but it was fine with us, we were just happy we could still do the race. It was so much fun running through all the parks and stopping to take pictures with characters. We had a blast, and we will never forget our first half marathon, we are hoping to do it again.

Later that night we all went to Universal Studios and Epcot. We walked around and did some easy rides. I really didn't want to get out of my chair. I was tired, but overall, we all had a great time.

Mike was leaving us early in the morning, we had such a great time running the Princess Race. We both were left with such great memories.

Our next part of the trip we were going to Daytona Beach and staying right on the beach. We were leaving Disney and waiting for our accessible Van to be dropped off.

Guess what, it never came, mom called the rental place and said the van had not been dropped off yet, and they still had to clean it before it reached us. We were not happy.

Luckily our key to our room still worked so we all went back to our room and called for a late checkout. Luckily Disney said we could have the room until 2 PM.

Lenny called the airport and said he would be down for the rental and wait for it. We were hoping this would save some time. Two O'clock was fast approaching and Lenny called to say he had the van and he was on his way to pick us up.

Finally, we were on our way to Daytona, we were all excited, we had our rental handicap van.

We arrived at our hotel. It was gorgeous, we loved our condo with a kitchenette, one big bedroom, a huge bathroom, and we were right on the ocean. But guess what, no hospital bed! Mom immediately called the company and asked if it was coming? The company said no, they didn't know what happened and they would send us one that night, or the next day. Mom was furious, we needed that bed immediately, I had no bed.

We waited and waited and no bed, we were missing our vacation time. There was a pullout couch in the room that Lenny made into a bed, and I used that for the night. Mom made sure it was comfortable enough for me.

We went off to the beach, and for the first time ever I had freedom to ride my motorized wheelchair on the beach. I LOVED IT!

It was winter break for college students, so mom and I went over and talked to the kids, and they all sang me a song and circled around me. I met some gorgeous looking girls; I was in heaven! I couldn't stop smiling!

We went to eat at Bubba Gump Shrimp Restaurant, it was our first time for all of us. I was so excited about my drink it was a Corona beer tipped over in a margarita, called a Coronarita. It was so big I didn't finish it.

By the time we got back to our hotel, the hospital bed still never arrived, and they said it would be brought the next day. Mom wasn't too happy!

Thank god I did well on the pull out bed on the couch, hopefully my bed will arrive for tonight. We went off to the beach again and I loved how we could drive our van right on the hard sand. The sand was very compact, so it is perfect for my motorized wheelchair. I just rode my chair on a fast speed and Lenny and mom were trying to keep up with me.

I felt free, and loved to look at the ocean, I told mom I wanted to come back every year. It was a nice break from the cold weather; my body was in less pain.

Soon nighttime came, and luckily my hospital bed arrived for our last two nights.

I was able to experience Bike week, I loved it especially all the women. So many bikers, and different bikes. We had a great time in Daytona and we all can't wait to go back again.

We rode back to Orlando to finish up our last five days, and my sister Kimberly and her boyfriend Kyle came down to visit. Our hotel was beautiful with a pool. I had my own room with a regular bed.

We went to SeaWorld and toured their Penguin habitat and pet a penguin. It was freezing on that tour, but it was very interesting. I loved the shows.

We went to Alligator Land, and I held a baby alligator and had a snake around my neck to take a picture. Mom and I even went to feed about thirty alligators up close, Lenny thought we were crazy, he stayed back. It was interesting.

We all went to Discovery Cove. While we were getting checked in, a manager was nearby and he upgraded us to a Private Cabana.

This meant free towel service, snack basket, mini fridge stocked with cola products and water. Liquor was free and they had great food.

We all had to put on wet suits; this was extremely hard to put on me. We all did the swim with the dolphin experience, we loved it, the staff was so good, and they even held me in the water and told the others to enjoy themselves.

We took many pictures and purchased them at the end. It was a great experience for us all. I loved the bird encounter and feeding them. Swimming with stingrays, baby sharks and other fish it was very interesting.

I loved having Kyle and Kim with us, it made it more fun for me. I missed Kim when she left to go back home, because it was nice to have her help me with my morning and nightly routine. It was like the old days when she lived at home.

Lenny, mom and I went to the Kennedy Space Center; I had a nicer time than I thought I would have. I loved to see the Atlantis, I met an astronaut, and we even bought space food. I loved the movie attraction the most, I got to see how they live in space, it was so amazing, I watched it twice. I would love to go back and go to the launching pad. It was very interesting.

I had to say we had the best vacation, I had so many first-time experiences, and I can't wait to come back again. I am a lucky guy to have a family that gives me these adventures and allows me to live life to the fullest.

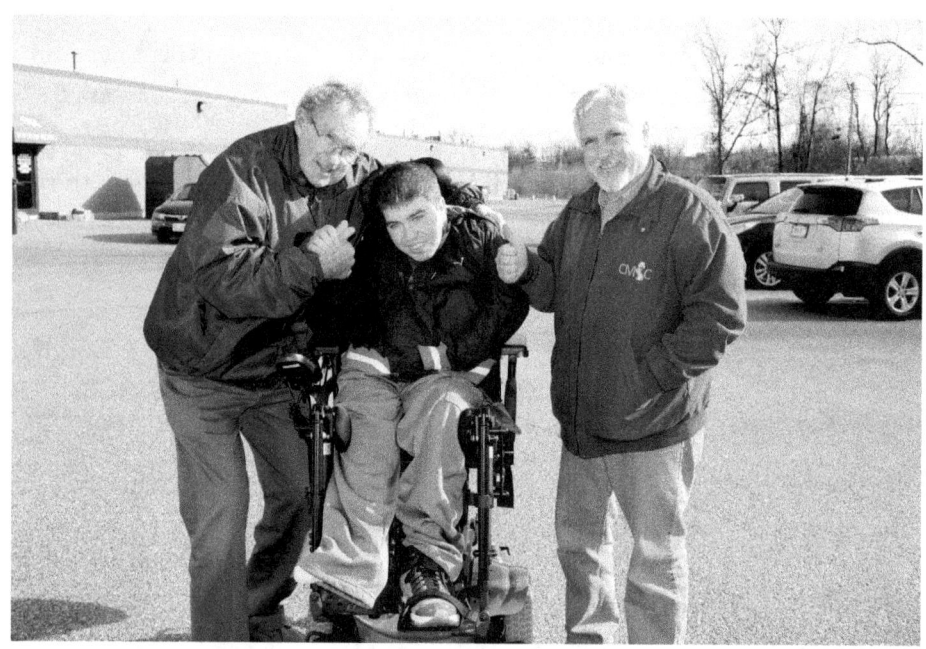

Tim Cooney and Don Sampson from CMSC Driving School
let Kyle drive an accessible van, 2016

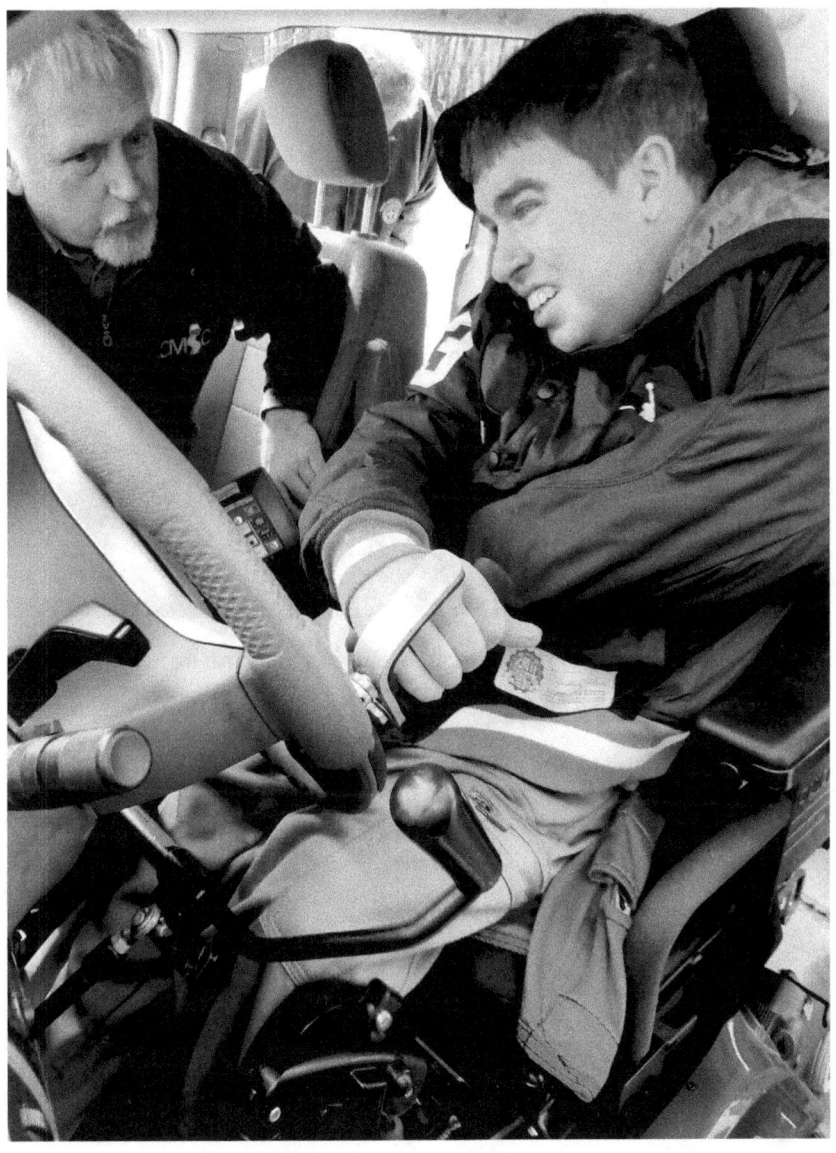

Don Sampson, driving instructor, helping Kyle to drive, 2016

Michael DiDonato and Kyle finished the Half Marathon Princess race in Walt Disney World, Orlando, FL, 2016

Chapter Seven

The day for my surgery is only a few days away, it has come so fast. Soon the infective hardware on my spine will be removed and I will be free from this infection in my body that I have had for a few years.

This week has been filled with so much love and good wishes from so many people. Friends and family were all coming over to wish me good luck.

It became kind of crazy, so my mother said, "Why don't I just post on Facebook that you will be at the Kahula Restaurant tonight. If anyone wants to stop by and wish you well, they can."

I gave mom a huge smile and said, "It sounds great to me", and my thumb was up.

It turned out to be an amazing night, so many people came that I haven't seen in a long time. I had so much fun! I really felt the love and new that so many people really cared about me.

That night when I was put to bed, I said thank you to Lenny and mom for always giving me the best of times.

Mom said, "You deserve it, you have been through so much, you have so many people that LOVE you, and pray for you all the time."

That night I fell asleep, and I did feel happy and loved!

The next morning waking up, I said, "Mom, why does everyone act like I'm going to die, it's like it's the last time they will see me?"

Mom said, "They know that this is a huge surgery, they want you to know you are loved, and they are praying for you".

"Everyone knows how strong you are, and you always beat everything you have been through. They are all cheering you on, they care about you"!

I am not going to DIE; I will survive this and show everyone! I still have a lot of living to do and I want my big 30th Birthday bash.

Mom just smiled and said, "We will start planning it when you have recovered some, don't worry, you will have a party."

Lenny and Mom, went out for a bit, I asked, "Where are you going"?

"We are going to Saint Anne's Shrine; I want to light a candle for you and daddy!

I said, "Thank you."

I know this is something mom does for me before every major surgery.

I could tell when mom came home, she was crying, she was scared, but her being mom and always being strong in front of me she said, "She was fine."

Morning soon came, I wanted to wear my Batman pajama bottoms with my Karate Kid t-shirt, my awesome socks, and my black belt from karate.

I said to mom, I am ready to kick this surgeries ass, just like I have done every other one.

She said, "I have no doubt you will. You are so strong."

Mom got me dressed and off to the hospital we went.

My family and my friend Cynthia all came to the hospital with me, this time it was different, I wasn't brought to the normal pre-op room before surgery. I was brought to another room that had a lot of privacy.

Dr. Nimec, Dr. Glotzbecker my surgeon, and the Anesthesiologist were there. I have to say the mood was very serious, and mom was talking to them on the side. I tried not to focus on the severity of the surgery because I knew I didn't have a choice. If I wanted a chance at living, I had to take this chance and do this surgery. My biggest concern was making sure I had my little bear that always comes with me into surgery. I always request the lemonade flavor to put me to sleep. These were my good luck charms, and I would always have my father with me.

My family kept me laughing till it was time to go, mom came into the surgical room with me all dressed in surgical scrubs. She held my hand, and we talked about karate and listened to daddy's CD of him singing. Mom telling me everything was going to be fine and when I feel better, we will be planning your birthday bash.

She said, "I love you," and I was off to sleep.

After a long 14 hours of surgery it was done, my hardware was taken out. I am in the ICU to recover. I still have the breathing tube in me for the next twenty-four hours, then it will be pulled if I am breathing on my own and stable. I have drains, helping the infection to drain out and I am on several antibiotics. Now we hope the infection will heal and my blood work will have some great results.

The next day, in the early afternoon the nurse was able to pull my tube out. My mom was with me, and she was holding my hand and the first thing I said was.

"Can we plan my 30th Birthday Bash?" Mom smiled and she said, "We sure can".

Mom said, "Kyle you did great, you surprised everyone once again, you did it in one surgery.

The doctor was very pleased on how you didn't lose a lot of blood and how my body handled taking out all the hardware. They expected you to have three to five surgeries to complete the operation, but you did so well that they could complete it in one surgery.

Dr. Glotzbecker stated that I was his oldest patient he ever operated on, and I was extremely strong, and tough. The Dr. stated the infection was very bad as he thought, and I made the best decision to have the procedure.

The doctor stated, I was the most difficult person to position for surgery that he has ever had, and he hopes to never have to operate on me again, with a smile! "

My baclofen pump is infected so my next surgery will be in five days to replace it. My shunts are not infected so that is a relief. I did amazing after my spine surgery, I was surprisingly up in my wheelchair eating in the cafeteria a few days after. My doctor was shocked, and he even came to find me to see if I was there and eating. He told me "I never met anyone like you," with a smile!

It was time for my Baclofen pump surgery, this surgery is a tough one because now they are taking the catheter out and putting a new pump and catheter in. My new pump will be filled with baclofen and then programed to give me bolus feeds, to catch me up with the meds I lost.

It was a nightmare; after the anesthesia worn off me, I was in extreme pain with spasms. This surgery was harder on me than taking out the hardware from my spine. It took several days to get my meds adjusted to where they needed to be. Boy did I suffer. I went through severe withdrawals, my spasms were so bad, I wanted to die.

My mom kept telling the baclofen pump team what they needed to do, but they didn't want to be as aggressive as she suggested. The team of doctors were worried that it could affect me with my heart. They would only do bolus feeds in baby steps, so that's why I suffered so much.

Mom kept telling them to look at my old medical records, and they would see that I could handle bolus feeds fine, or they could call my other doctors. We have done this numerous times, and you need to stop making him suffer.

My withdrawals from the baclofen, made me sweat, it only took minutes for my sheets and hospital gown to be soaked. I was spasming, my body was out of control and the other meds they were giving me, did not touch me. Mom wouldn't stop fighting for me until they listened to her. She told the doctor if they didn't call, she would.

Finally, the doctor's listened and called my other doctor, and she came in to see me and soon after my bolus feeds were increased more often to get me where I needed to be.

Know I was finally starting to feel better. We were able to go home in the next day or so with a picc line to continue my antibiotics for six months to a year. My mom had to learn how to give my meds through a picc line and I also had some nursing care to check on me a couple times a week. My infection is going down which is great news.

Being home and not in all that pain was such a relief. Now, I want to plan my birthday bash. Mom has a lot to do. I would like the biggest party ever! I am alive and I want to celebrate!

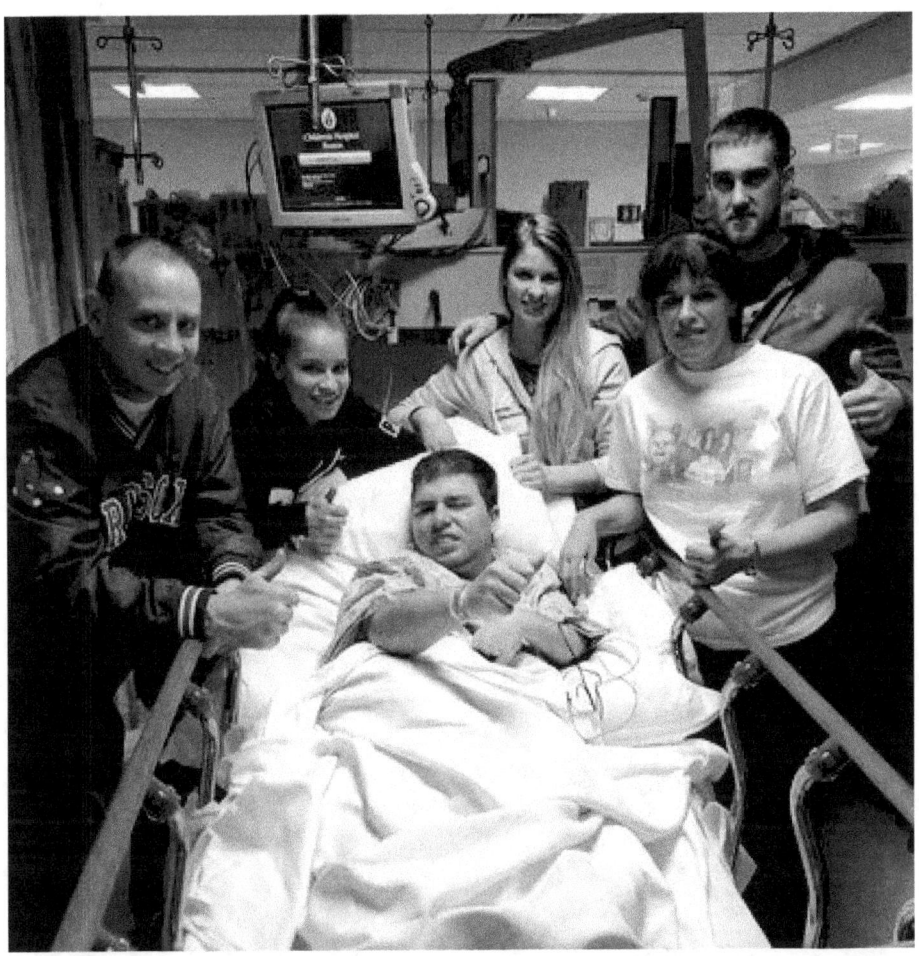

My family with me in pre-op before my Spinal Fusion removal surgery, 2016

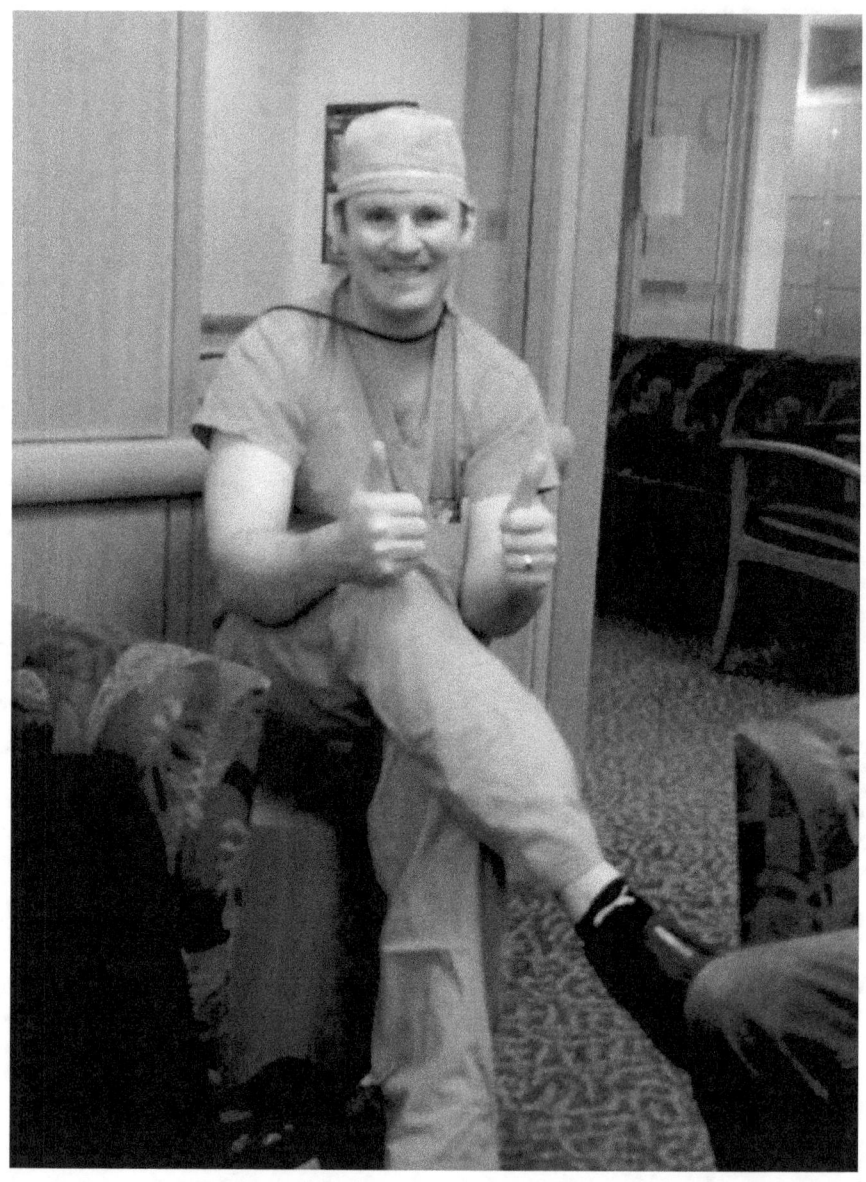

Dr. Michael Glotzbecker who saved my life
and removed all my infected spinal fusion hardware, 2016

If I Can Smile, I Can Live

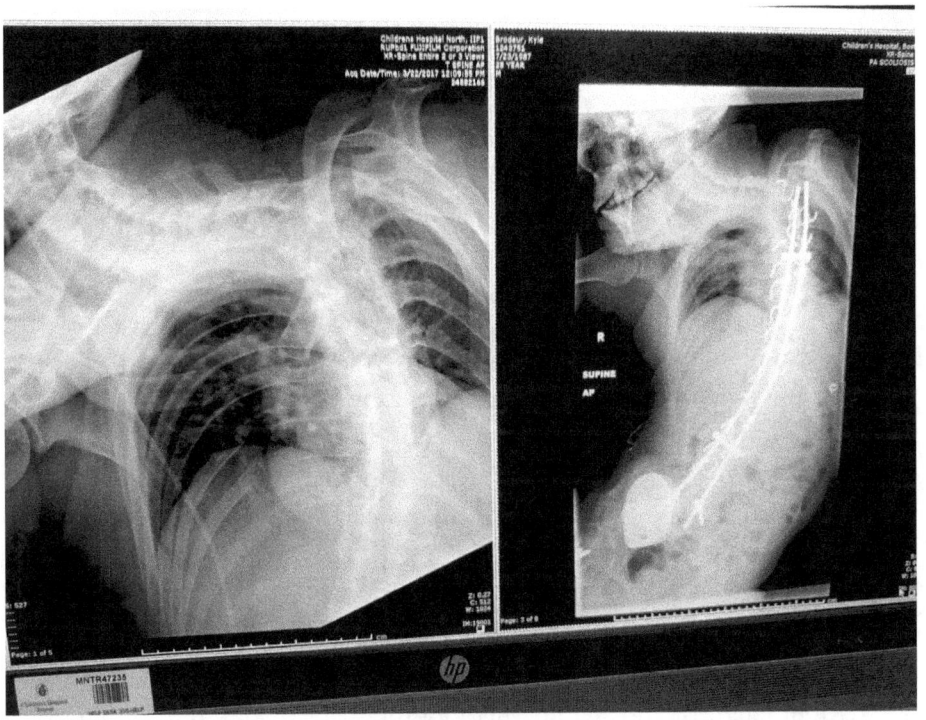

X-ray of hardware removed from my spine, before and after, 2016

Chapter Eight

Planning my birthday bash was so much fun, Mom said I can have whatever I wanted. Boy did she regret saying that, when I told her I wanted a Las Vegas Party, with Vegas girls!

Mom said, "Vegas girls, oh boy, who would do that? I am sure your sisters wouldn't."

I said "You and your friends will."

Mom said "me? I wouldn't even know what to do and I doubt my friends would, we are all in our fifties now. We would make a fool of ourselves."

I said, "Ask Evelyn, she will."

Mom laughed, and she text her and told her my idea and Evelyn said, "I'm in, that sounds like fun."

Mom was shocked, so now I have her really considering it and trying to figure out what friends would do this for me.

She immediately asked her group of friends that came on our pontoon boat if they would be Vegas girls at my birthday bash. One by one, her phone was beeping back, saying they would love to, but only for Kyle, and how much fun this would be.

The girls started talking about Vegas costumes and figuring out ideas of a dance. Mom couldn't believe what she just got herself into.

The Vegas girls all got together to talk about costumes and a dance. Mom decided to ask Tina Gagnon who owned a dance studio to help teach all the girls a Vegas dance. Tina responded and she was happy to assist us ladies and try to make us a Vegas dance routine.

Every week the girls got together for about three months learning a dance. I could tell my mother was having fun; and enjoyed it, she loved dance night!

Since I was having a Vegas show, Frank Damelio volunteered to do a magic show, after all what is a Vegas Night without magic.

We decided we would have a few speakers, and have appetizers for food, lots of decorations, music and a Las Vegas show girl Cake! I also asked to have a video made. Of course, mom said yes to whatever I wanted. Now we need to find vendors to help make this night a success. Then whom are we inviting to this big bash?

Mom wasted no time, we found a hall that we could provide the food, a DJ Wayne Raymond offered his services, mom found Loren Stanard to make me a Vegas dancer cake, and she hired a balloon decorator, Amazing Balloons. We hired a Video vendor, Michael Montigny, everything was in place but the invites.

Mom said, "This party was so special and so much love for you that we should just make it a Facebook event."

So that's what we did, we really didn't know who would attend.

Two months before our event was to take place my mom went to the hall and when she spoke to the women in charge, she said it wasn't listed that we had an event that day. Come to find out they double booked the same day, and we were left out of having a hall. It was a complete mess.

Mom was searching for a hall, and she called LaSalle Hall in Southbridge and they happened to have the date available. Only issue was, mom didn't want to have it catered, she wanted to supply the food and purchase some. Now she was stuck.

She had to go talk to Lenny Petrillo from Annie's Country kitchen, to see if he wouldn't mind not catering and just do the bar service, mom was nervous.

She went down to the restaurant, and he wasn't available so she talked to his wife and told her the situation, and she said she would talk to Lenny that night and have him call me.

That night we got a phone call from Lenny; I couldn't believe what he said to my mom. Lenny offered to donate all the food for my bash, and he would offer a cash bar. My mom didn't know what to say, she thanked him and was taken by his generosity.

It was above and beyond, and she stressed that she wouldn't mind making some food and ordering some appetizers from him.

Lenny insisted that he wanted to cater it for me, and he was honored to be part of such an event. My mom gave me the phone so Lenny could tell me himself that we could use the LaSalle Hall for my birthday bash and said he would love to caterer it. I had a huge smile on my face, knowing my wish was going to happen.

Together mom and I made a Facebook event inviting so many people that followed me on my sport page and regular Facebook. Now we wait to see if people would want to attend. We were shocked at the responses of so many attending. We knew we could have at least two hundred people attend to celebrate with me.

The day before my bash was very busy, mom was doing so much baking; she had to go to the hall to set up and my Vegas girls had to do a trial run on the stage. Even though it was a crazy day we were all so excited. There were so many beautiful decorations, even a kissing booth that I had to have. I had to say everything looked perfect.

The big day had arrived; I had my Vegas shirt on, and lots of different hats and costume accessories to take pictures with. Tables were all decorated, and the hall was full of Balloons. Gold balloons spelling KYLE up high across the stage, and a slot machine for cards, my kissing booth all decorated, and the entrance was beautiful, decorated with balloons and big Cards. I even had a table with pictures and one with my father, and goose feathers.

It was perfect; I never thought it would look like this. The caterer had all the tables set up for the buffet in the middle of the floor and my gorgeous Vegas Show Girl cake was amazing! Now all we need is the people!

Everyone started to show up, some I didn't know, they all came to wish me a happy birthday!

We had 200 to 250 people throughout the night.

I never thought this many people would actually want to come to my party.

My Vegas show was a hit, my magician did an amazing job, and everyone loved his tricks, my mom had a surprise for me, she had Monique Vacon sing me "Hero" song, that was special to me.

Lastly my Vegas girls, all my dancers. I know they did the best they could, they were nervous, they had a few mess-ups, but they pulled it off for me and I loved it.

I also had three speakers, Tessi from my old school that use to take care of me, Tim from CMSC driving school, and Mike my teammate with Team Unstoppable. They all spoke of memories with me, and how I change their life.

My mom thanked the vendors and everyone that came to wish me a Happy Birthday.

She told the audience "Kyle is so happy, because of all of you, you make him feel loved and wanted, it takes a tribe to raise my son.

Thank you from the bottom of my heart! "

Then we sang Happy Birthday!

I have to say my favorite part of the night was my kissing booth, getting kisses and taking pictures with everyone that came. It made me special memories that I will never forget.

I am thankful for my DVD of my party. I always laugh when my Vegas girls go on the stage, the mess-ups are so funny, I love to watch it.

The tape makes me smile and I love watching the night over and over again.

Mom always says this was like a wedding, a huge birthday bash full of love! I have to say she is correct!

Now I can't wait for another birthday bash!

My stepfather Lenny, Mom and I, 2017

If I Can Smile, I Can Live

My Vegas Girls dancers at my 30th Birthday Party, 2017

My special friend Page, and me, 2017

Chapter Nine

I have so much excitement happening all the time and so much to look forward to that I get my body so stressed. My family always tells me, I must calm down. My heart rate goes up, my breathing goes down, I turn purple, I start to sweat, and my spasms get unbearable.

I now have a Hiatal Hernia and have had three small bowel obstructions. I need to learn to stay calm but my muscle tone has been getting worse.

I have to admit, it's nice having sister's that are nurses and a physician assistant, now I have many people looking over me besides my mother. A few years back, my mom had back surgery and the next day I ended up in the Emergency room. Thank God I had my sisters, Katie rode with me in the ambulance and Kim and Katie took turns staying with me at the hospital. They took really good care of me. It was very hard on my mom not being able to be with me.

Katie was with me in the ER, when my blood work came back initially, they said I had necrotizing fasciitis which is serious, Katie called my mother and was very concerned. Mom was helpless she just had surgery the day before. Soon after a doctor came in and ruled out that diagnosis, and said I had a peri anal abscess. At least this was not as serious.

I was admitted and given antibiotics, and my abscess had to be packed twice a day. It was extremely hard, I only had one PCA at the time. Mom found a way to pack my abscess and give me the care needed.

It took a few weeks for the abscess to heal, then I was all set once again.

Another time I had to be taken by ambulance to the hospital, I was vomiting bile, mom couldn't ride with me in the ambulance cause of COVID.

While on our way to the hospital we rode by our crash on Route 20, and a deer jumped over the guardrail and crashed into our ambulance.

The EMT that was with me went flying, he hurt his shoulder. The driver was okay thankfully. I was okay but a little nervous. We continued to the hospital.

I can't believe this happened where our crash was twenty-three years ago.

I arrived at the hospital and mom wasn't allowed in to be with me. She called a few times and each time they said NO! It didn't matter that I was paralyzed and have a Traumatic Brain Injury. These Covid restrictions need to be changed! I wasn't happy.

The nurse kept calling mom to ask questions about me and she kept saying,

"I am in the parking lot, please let me in. I am more help to you inside helping to care for Kyle. You don't know his body and he will stress more if he isn't positioned correctly."

Again, she was told she had to wait. Which made no sense.

Eventually my mother was let in, after ninety minutes. I felt better and could relax more, because mom will be my voice and advocate for me.

Now they want blood from me, they can draw blood but it's always difficult placing an IV in me. After several tries, they finally get an IV, the problem is they never last long.

I had a CT Scan done and it showed I have a small bowel obstruction from my scar tissue. I had to have an NG tube put in my nose, and I hated that. I ended up pulling it out on the third day. Mom wasn't too happy with me. I know I shouldn't pull it out but I do know when I feel better. I tend to get an obstruction once a year now. I am thankful it cleared up fast. We were released to go home after three days.

I have been fortunate to ride on snowmobiles, Tubing, parasailing, rollercoaster's, waterslides. Yes, you read it correctly all these experiences I have had. I have to say it is a challenge and sometimes scary, but I love it! It is worth taking chances so I can experience life. Luckily, I have a great stepfather, Lenny has always lifted or carried me, to do everything I want to experience.

One person asked me if I would ever like to go up in a spaceship? The answer is yes. It would be neat letting the gravity float me around.

This is one thing that would never happen though, besides, my body couldn't handle it. I have tried space food, and it's okay. I had the privilege to meet an astronaut and obtain his signature while I visited the space center in Florida.

If something ever happened to me while taking chances, I would never blame anyone, I am just thankful that I get these opportunities and I am not treated like I can't do anything because I am paralyzed.

It's very easy when you are so injured and in so much pain to give up or think that your life is over. I for one can tell you it's not, you must be willing to enjoy life still and find new ways of doing what makes you happy. I was fortunate enough to have a mother that never let me give up, she is my motivator, and she doesn't know how to say NO to me, which I love. Believe me she tries to say NO plenty of times, but my smile always wins!

My advise to someone that is injured. Don't look at what you don't have any longer, focus on what you do have and run with it.

It's okay to cry, life is hard, but we have to try to accept what is given us and live the best life we can.

Unfortunately we don't get second chances, so we need to make the best of what we have.

I try to not let myself get depressed any longer, every year around our anniversary November 1st, I would always act out and get myself in trouble especially at my school that I loved. I would go to counseling and talk about my feelings and emotions about loosing my father and my independence.

It's hard to accept all my losses in life, but I really don't have a choice. I do still hope that someday I will walk again, but I do realize that it may never happen, but I will never stop dreaming of it. It's been Twenty-six years since I have walked.

I do remember the feeling of independence I once had. I can't help but miss it, but I had to accept that my independence is no longer and know I need help for everything I need to do. This can be very difficult at times, especially if I have an itch and no one is in my room to itch me. Thankfully my mother's bedroom is close by and if I yell to her, she can come to my rescue.

There are times however that I may need help late at night, but I am too tired to use my voice for help. My mother has no idea that I needed to be changed or if I vomited.

Morning arrives and my mother comes in and if I vomited, she feels so bad that I sat in it all night and she always says,

"Why didn't you just say, Mom, I need you"? Thank god this doesn't happen often.

One thing that really aggravates me is when my I-Pad goes off and I can't get up to see who called or left me a message. Now mom will shut it off completely, so I don't know what I am missing. My I-Pad is my voice, my communication. I love how I can message on it and talk to my friends or family.

I know sometimes I can be a pain and make facetime calls, but I can't help it. This aggravates my mom so much. She will take the I-Pad away from me. She doesn't want me to bother people.

The only limb on my body that works is my right arm, this one arm allows me to drive my motorized chair, feed myself if I have the energy and I'm not lazy.

I love to stretch in bed by holding my bed rails, arm wrestle, use my communication device (I-Pad), use my bee-bee gun, pet my dog Allie or other animals, hold babies, play games and most importantly hug and hold hands with all the beautiful ladies I meet.

Even though I have one arm, I cannot wash myself or use it to a degree of lifting my body or to use a manual chair. I have limited use because of my muscle tone and curvatures throughout my body. I have no trunk control, or any control over my body, I am paralyzed. Thank god I have PCA's, Lenny or my mother to help me for every need I may have.

How do I survive all of this? You need a sense of humor; you need to have people in your life that are silly and fun. You can't be a stressed person; I don't like to be around negativity or people that dwell on there little problems. I will always set them straight and let them know it could be a lot worse, they could have my life and struggles. I also know I am lucky; I could have it much worse.

If I Can Smile, I Can Live

I have had many surgeries and procedures to date and I know I have many more coming my way. I live for today, and the good of what's ahead, I refuse to focus on the medical and bumps in the road that I may have.

When I go to doctor's appointments and hear bad news, I have to forget about it and not focus on it. Of course it bothers me and stresses me out but for some reason my mother and I handle this stress in a different manner. We tend to joke a lot and just always say it will all work out in the end.

My body is difficult, and I am a huge challenge, but I also know I have made it through thirty-two surgeries, and should have never survived, I am a miracle. I am still here and have a lot of fight in me, and the will to live. I'm not ready to stop living.

Some people will say how can you always have a smile on your face?

My smile comes from being surrounded by great people. Thankfully I have family and friends that love me and take the time to make me feel special. I feel so lucky at times.

My family brings me so much happiness and especially my sister's and their husbands.

My sisters are older now; before they were married, they took me out with their friends at night on special occasions. It felt great to not have to go out with my mother!

Now my sisters have children, so life has changed but I love being an uncle. As of now I have two nephews, four nieces and one on the way, which is a boy.

All of them love helping me use my Barrier Free Lift. They get to press the button to lift me up or put me down.

They love my motorized wheelchair; mom gives them rides in it. I love to play with them, weather its with kids foam soap, string spray, water guns, high five or whatever we can think of. I love watching them grow up and now attending their sports and preschool graduations. These little humans are one of the best gifts I will ever receive especially because I will never have my own children.

Mom and I, our always shopping for the kids, I love to pick out special toys and activities for them.

I love when my friends treat me like the guys, I may be in a wheelchair but it doesn't mean I want to be treated any different from anyone else. I hate to be babied, that is one thing my family does not do. Yes, I do get yelled at. Mom doesn't yell often unless I really get her mad and that would be when I smash into a wall or I call her chubs. She hates that nickname, I try so hard not to call her that but sometimes it just comes out, you can say it's a very bad habit.

One thing that really gets me, is when people are talking to me that don't know me well, and they think that I can't hear them. They tend to talk loud, I tend to look at whom I am with, and smile because it's hilarious to me.

Just because someone is in a wheelchair doesn't mean they can't hear. I recommend to just to say "Hi "to the person in a normal voice and treat them like you would everyone else.

You will soon find out if the person can't talk or hear you.

In my case I can hear, but I don't have the air or energy to be vocal so I would have to use my speech device at that time. Some people don't have the patience and don't want to wait for me to spell everything out, so those people miss out on getting to know the real Kyle. There are times when I am tired and don't want to communicate but that is when my caregiver always helps me out.

I have two things in life that are hard for me to accept.

One is not being able to walk ever again. I have accepted it, I have adjusted to it, but it doesn't mean I can't hope for a miracle someday.

My other is having a real relationship with a woman. I have so many women around me, that I really enjoy being with, and do wish they were my real girlfriend. They all say they are, but really, they are not. I always meet their boyfriends and then eventually see them get married.

It's hard for me because I know they love me and care for me, but not in the way I want to be loved and cared for.

I wish I had my person; I would love to go out and purchase a diamond for a special woman in my life and plan a wedding and get married.

Of course, I want a family, my own children, I can't help but wonder. But never say never, lets hope it will happen.

I watch my sister's, friends and cousins all moving on in life, going to college or finding a job and planning their wedding. These are all things I can only wish for. I have to say I do envy them and even though I wish this was me I am very happy for them.

I am lucky enough that everyone that is in my life, always makes me a part of their life, I am never left out. So, do I enjoy these weddings, graduations, and seeing everyone move on with their lives? Yes, I do, and it's all because they make me feel so special and important.

Chapter Ten

Some of the joys of life that I wish I were able to do are mostly all the things we take for granted. I would love to know the feeling again on what's it like to put two feet on the ground, be able to walk, go to the bathroom and use a toilet again.

The feelings of standing in a shower, washing myself, touch my legs and clean my feet. I would love to just put my clothes on my own body.

The freedom just to bend over and tie my sneakers, get up from a chair, to change position in bed, to bend my legs, or to simply itch myself.

I miss the feeling of wearing two sneakers again on each foot, to play sports, kick, run and play with my nephews and nieces. I loved so many things in life that I could never do again.

I often wonder what it would be like to drive and get in and out of a truck, go to work every day, have a girlfriend, be married and have children. What would it be like to feel close to a woman?

I was ten years old when my school days were over in a public school system, I would give anything to take a test or have homework again and be with all my friends getting in trouble. If only I had another chance at life. I missed out on so much especially in my high school years, playing sports, dating, and just doing all the guy stuff. It's endless of so many losses in my life.

Be thankful you can do all these simple things, most of you take it for granted and not even think about not having it until you don't have it, then it's a real wake- up call.

If you have your health and freedom to move your body, you are one lucky person. Enjoy it, don't abuse it especially with drugs and alcohol.

Go make something of yourself, go to college or a trade school and make yourself a great life for you and your future family. If you can't figure out what you want to be in life, try different things. Go to different businesses, hospitals and hang out for the day and see if something interest you. Don't give up and settle, you need to be happy to make it in this crazy world.

I always wanted to have my own home, but it wouldn't be possible. I realize finding a PCA for 24 hour care would never happen. Besides, Mass Health doesn't cover that, I would need to go to a group home. If I wake up in the middle of the night and need a position change, or a brief change, who will do it?

I will suffer until morning comes and what happens if my caregiver doesn't show up?

It's not like I can talk and grab a cell phone and call someone for help. What happens if I want some food or a drink?

I guess I would have to starve and be thirsty.

I need someone to give me my morning and night medicine, I would be in seizures or severe pain without them.

Lots of times my eyes are itchy and burning, I need a cold towel, if no one is there then I would have to suffer it out, and believe me this is irritating, I can't take it. There are so many things that can go wrong medically or if there was a fire, or if someone broke in, what would I do?

So many worries that I know I am much better staying at home. I will never know that kind of independence.

I am witnessing my friends going on with their lives, finishing college, going to trade school and now married and starting their own families. I have to say I do wish I had all that also, especially my own family, I would have loved to be a father and make my mother a grandmother. I would be a great father and be like my father Michael; he was always there for all of us and showed me unconditional love by adopting me and giving me his last name. I miss him and think of him often. I don't think there is a day where I don't think of him.

My mom was getting me ready like she does every morning and she said,

"Life is like a bunch of chocolates you never know what you're going to get". and she said what kind of mother do you think you have? "A good or bad chocolate?

I said, "The best chocolate" Oh, did she like that, she said, "I made her day, and gave me a hug".

One thing for sure is I am very dependent on my family or my Personal Care Attendant. If my PCA doesn't come in; Lenny and my mom take over to make sure my needs are meant. I have been blessed with great care so far. When it comes to my caregiver's I love to have women especially when it comes to bathing me. I don't want a man to wash me. I do however like a male to take me out, have guy talk and do stuff, like going to look at dirt bikes, snowmobiles, and motorcycles. I love to watch the guys ride their toys. I would give anything to be able to do this. I really do envy them and I wish it was me but unfortunately, I know my body won't allow me to do this. But I can dream and get the thrill out of watching them.

I really wish I could shovel the snow or work a plow. I would have a big truck. There are times the driveway needs to be done and I wish I could go do it.

I was fortunate enough to get an Action Track Chair, with a plow, I loved using it in the woods and in the snow. I loved being in the woods and helping Lenny around the yard and plowing the snow.

Unfortunately, my body has curved more and going over the bumps brought my body into more spasms. We were looking into better shocks, but it can't be done to this chair. I only use it now on non-rocky surfaces.

There are so many wishes in life I wish I could do but I know realistically it just can't be. I choose not to sit around and dwell on it because if I do, I won't make it. I would be so depressed. My mother has installed in me that we can't look at what we don't have any longer and look at what we do have.

Let's look at what I can do!

I can LOVE, Feel, Taste, Eat, Smell, Hear, and I have my Vision! That alone is huge!

I am an artist, with my mom's assistance. It's a two-person effort, but I am still an artist. It doesn't matter how I do it, in the end I created it, and I am proud of it.

I am an athlete, running with Mike, Team Unstoppable, which I love going fast and feeling the wind when we do the bike portion in our races, we participate in.

I love being an uncle and watching all six of them grow up. I love playing with them, they make me happy.

I go out to eat at restaurants, I enjoy having a drink and I love desert. Thankfully I have a good size family that I get to visit. I enjoy boating and fishing. I love campfires and toasting marshmallows. I love to go in the water if I have a beautiful girl holding me. As I am getting older, I don't like the cold water any longer, I will only go in if it's around 90 degrees. I do prefer a hot tub now, but because of my Baclofen pump the water can't be more than 100 degrees.

I love my I-pad, you tube, movies, face timing. I enjoy the outside, especially rolling on flat trails where I can have the freedom with my chair and go the speed I want. I am always restricted on speed especially in my house or in any social environment. If I am in a crowded area, I will tend to hit walls or run people over. My muscle tone is so severe I can hardly move my neck. I favor the right side; I have a left side neglect.

My biggest blessing in life is my immediate family; they show and give me love unconditionally. They understand me even at times when I can't speak, and this is often. I have to say they know me very well and they can always figure out what I need or want. What I love most is we don't have a grumpy house; I know I am loved. I tend to get very lazy at times. I don't want to do anything for myself. This irritates my mother, and she lets me know how she feels. She would tell me I was lazy and my father wouldn't like this. She also reminds me, that there our people that wish they had one arm to do the things that I can do, so stop saying I WILL and DO IT!!

I do feel loved and that is what matters most. I think at times my mom loves me too much, but I do realize she is mom and just wants the best for me. I know it's good that I have someone that motivates me to keep going and to never give up. We all need that person, and I know I keep my mother going also.

A PCA asked me who my best friend was, and I said, "My mom", and mom was shocked, she said, "I have never asked him that question before. Wow, I am your best friend and Kyle is my best friend too."

Mom always says, I know her the best out of anyone, and I know that is true. We spend so much time together.

Some things we just take for granted but I am glad we both know now.

Chapter Eleven

I am asked: Do I have survivor's guilt?
My answer is No, I do not, and the reason behind it is, I wouldn't want my father to suffer the way I do.

Our crash was head on, my father would be in tough shape, and he would have never been able to lead a life full of happiness like he had. I really don't think he would have handled being paralyzed and having mom take care of him. I am happy for him that he didn't experience this kind of pain but sad that he is not enjoying life with our family.

I do believe my father sent me back to my mother and sister's. He always said, when he wasn't around, I was in charge.

I was near death; mom was holding my hand while my body was shutting down.

My body started to show improvement on the monitors after my mom told me,

"This was it, you must decide, if you want to stay with your sisters and I and if you do, she promised to never leave me and be by my side always. If I decided to go with daddy that was okay also, she knew I would be okay."

Shortly after that, my body started to come back. The monitors were showing progress, it was a miracle, my mom said.

The doctor's said, "I wouldn't make the night."

I had several surgeries and everything that could go wrong did. I finally started breathing and was taken off the ventilator after seven long weeks.

I truly believe that my father wanted me here to take care of my mother and sister's. My mother couldn't bare losing a child after losing a husband. I helped my mom and helped her to stay focused and strong and raising us kids.

I know you're thinking how did I do this, take care of my mother and sisters? I kept my mom's mind so busy thinking of how to get me better and trying to take care of my sister's in between her crazy schedule with so many appointments.

She didn't have much alone time, and time for herself. All her energy and time was trying to make us kids happy in between all the surgeries and hospital visits.

There were times my mom would cry, and I would see her wiping her tears, and I always told her.

"Dad is so proud of you".

She would come in bed and lay with me and always tell me how happy she was to have me, and she could have never dealt with loosing me also!

I always said, "I no mom, that's why daddy sent me back! "

My mother and I understand each other. We keep each other motivated. We help each other when one is having a hard or bad day. We would be lost without one another. We our together every day, we know each other so well.

I helped with my little sister's. They were so busy trying to keep me happy. The girls would sing, play games, watch movies, dance for me to make me laugh. This helped my mom to get things done around the house. My sisters were helping me, but I was helping also, by keeping their mind busy and using their brain instead of just sitting around doing nothing.

I loved to watch home video's; the girls would watch them with me, and we would cuddle in my hospital bed. We have many DVDs of our family; this is a huge blessing to us all. We all know we had a very loving and caring father that did everything for us.

I went with my mother attending all my sister's events whether it was cheerleading or a school event. I also would tell my sister's if they were not behaving and to be good. I would never let them complain about school or if they had a backache or headache.

I always said do you want to be me? I would love to trade places with you, this would always keep them from complaining. I always told them to be thankful they can do all they do, because I can never again.

One of the biggest things I have done for my sister's and other's is teaching them about medical. I have had so much medically happen to me that my sister's became adjusted to hospitals and medical procedures at a very young age. They have learned IV's, wounds, therapies, and care for someone who cannot do anything for themselve.

They learned to appreciate life and to be thankful they can do everything and not be paralyzed. I taught them how to be compassionate and a great caregiver, now two of my sister's are nurses and one is a Physician Assistant. I have one sister in college majoring in Occupational Therapy. I am very proud of this and I know I taught them well. I bought each of my sister's their stethoscopes; I want them to carry me with them always.

I will continue to make my father proud and make sure I am always there for my sisters and my mother. I have to say it's not an easy job to take on, but I am doing my best. I do Love my family and I am very thankful for them.

I know at times I don't show it, but I am. I know I wouldn't be here if it wasn't for all the LOVE, they give me each day.

When I tell my mom I love her for no reason, she smiles and she always says, "I love you more! "

Sometimes she will say, "Did I tell you today that you our my favorite son?"

I always say, "No shit, I am your only son! " We both just laugh!

Chapter Twelve

How do you feel about forgiveness?

Can I forgive someone that took so much from me?

Can you forgive someone that made a choice to drink & drive and take cocaine?

Do I forgive someone for choosing not to have a designator driver?

Do I forgive someone that has never showed any remorse?

All I can say is that I don't have the time and energy to worry about someone that has never cared about my family and me. The effects of what this crash, did to my family you wouldn't wish on anyone. Some will say you have to forgive to have acceptance, but I say I have accepted what is given me and believe in God, but I don't have the time in my life to feel for someone that can't take responsibility for their own actions.

My mother and relatives have gone to court so many times and not once did Keith Doucette show any remorse, not one single tear.

The first time I was taken to court, I was only 11 years old. Immediately when Keith came in the courtroom in his handcuffs and shackles, I put up my middle finger to show my emotions.

I was in my wheelchair having spasms and my muscle tone was out of control, I was sweating badly. My mom tried to calm me down, but I was so upset for everything he has taken from me, and especially killing my father.

The district attorney came to get my mother and she left the court room, and she was told that Keith had decided to plead guilty. This met there will be no trial and he will be sentenced today.

Doucette pleaded guilty to manslaughter and the vehicular homicide charge would be dismissed.

So not fair for us! My father was killed on impact, I am paralyzed for life, and he gets to plead guilty, imagine that.

I wish it was that easy for my father and me. We don't get a chance to have our life back and we did nothing wrong.

My mother was told she could write a victim statement and she let Keith know all our hardships and all the challenges we were all going through. It was a lot to take in, I felt bad for myself but also for my sisters.

The girls were so young, only three and five years old when our crash happened. Kim had a lot of anxiety and speech problems; she missed our father so much and mom could hardly be home because she was always with me in the hospitals.

Katie had to relearn how to walk again, she was in a body cast for two months, and she screamed a lot from her pain and spasms in her legs. Mom would tell me how they missed their big brother; they wanted to know if I would ever be able to play with them again?

I told my mom to tell Keith "Don't drink and drive". Keith's face never changed, he heard so much that was taken from us, but it was like he didn't even care.

Keith was sentenced to only three to five years in a state prison, with ten years' probation to begin after his release. Conditions of probation included drug and alcohol evaluation and one hundred hours of community service a year. Keith was also ordered not to drive a car for seven years after he was released from prison.

Mom was shaking and crying as they took Keith away. We didn't see any emotion at all from Keith. I wondered if he even had a heart.

We had many hearings and court dates to attend through the years. Keith got released from prison on good behavior, he served three in half years.

After being on probation Keith got into trouble again, this time for obtaining a license illegally, speeding, and driving on the wrong side of the road. He had tested positive for cocaine use, and he hadn't been doing his community service.

I was excited when mom told me, because now, we had a chance for him to go back to prison and serve a longer sentence. This time hopefully for killing my father.

My sisters and I all wrote victim statements, mine took a long time I had to do it with my mother. I had so many feelings to share with him and what he took from me.

The day arrived when we all went to court, now my sisters and I are older. Katie was eleven,

Kim was thirteen, and I was nineteen, we were all so happy we finally will get to tell Keith ourselves how he forever changed our lives.

The last time I seen him I was still in a comatose state, now I am not, I want to get a good look at Keith. Kimberly and Katie wanted to understand why he didn't have any feelings or show any emotion.

"Doesn't he even care he took our daddy away from us?" Kimberly asked.

Judge John McCann was the affiliating judge. Judge McCann had reviewed the case and stated that Keith had several parole violations. Each violation was read aloud. Before he sentenced Mr. Doucette Judge McCann allowed our family to get up and speak one at a time.

My sister's told Keith and the Judge so many hardships that they go through with watching me suffer, and the fear that someday I might not come home from the hospital. They shared how hard it was to go to a friend's house and watch their friends play with their dads and watching them getting kisses and hugs.

They wished they still had that love from their father.

Our father will never see us graduate from school or give us away at our weddings or be a grandfather. They will never know this because of Keith being so irresponsible.

It was heart wrenching for me to hear of all their worries and special times they are missing.

I'm the oldest I suppose to be able to take care of my sisters and not have them worry about me.

Mom went up, she was shaking, and she was angry. She let Keith know how difficult life has been, and how I have had eighteen surgeries in eight years. The pain and suffering that we all have endured and it's never ending.

Our life is a life of struggles for us all. My husband is in a casket, he lost all enjoyments of life, and he was only thirty-nine years of age.

Mom said I have three children without a father, I am disabled now, and I live in a lot of pain, at times I can't walk. I am crawling to take care of my son who is paralyzed all because you CHOSE TO DRINK AND TAKE DRUGS THAT NIGHT!

Keith has been given several chances and has failed. He doesn't want to grow up, he makes his own rules. Keith committed manslaughter; he should go back to prison for killing my husband and get the help he needs.

Now it was my turn, Keith's attorney did not want me to go up. Thankfully the judge allowed it.

I was by my mom's side, and she read my statement.

Keith, "Eight years ago, all I asked from you was not to drink, drive or do drugs. But being the irresponsible person that you are, you did. You took everything from me, even my father. My life is so many surgeries and hospital procedures and stays. "Keith, you could never walk in my shoes even if you tried. You are too weak. You don't have the strength or courage that I have, or we wouldn't be here today.

I asked the judge to let him serve the rest of his probation time in prison, since this man took my father's life and my life also. I am in prison for the rest of my life, I don't get any second chances.

I thanked the judge, and my mom and I went back to our seats. I looked at Keith and gave him my middle finger gesture, since I had no voice.

The judge heard us loud and clear and before sentencing Judge McCann said,

"In my eleven and a half years as a judge, I have never seen such flagrant disregard for conditions of parole."

Then he sentenced Keith to serve nine to twelve years in prison for all six of his parole violations.

I had the biggest smile on my face, mom and my sisters were in tears, finally some justice. Keith will finally serve some time for killing our father.

I have lost and suffered tremendously in life, and I still do. I have watched my mother and sisters suffer emotionally and watch my mother suffer in pain trying to take care of me.

Through the years I have listened to my sister's cry for our father and seen my mother shed many tears of missing him and wishing dad was here.

There were times when I got so sad and angry my body went into spasms, I couldn't shed a tear like everyone else, I don't have tears. I couldn't even get up, out of my chair or bed to go hug my mother or sister's when they were crying or having a bad day, all I could do was open my eyes big and listen, I couldn't speak.

Yes, I was trapped in a body that couldn't respond to my loved ones, it was difficult.

After I came out of my coma and could stay alert and realize what was going on around me, I ached inside. I wanted to cuddle on the couch with my mom and sister's, I wanted so badly to play with my father on the floor, hide n seek, play sports, rollerblade, ride my bike, go to cub scouts, karate, go to school and be with my friends, instead I was in a hospital bed so fragile and trying to understand what happened and how did this happen. I was so envy of everyone around me, I want to walk and do what everyone else was doing.

It took me many years to understand and to not be angry and to accept my father was never coming back. My mom had to speak often to me about my injuries to make me understand why I couldn't do certain things. I even dreamed I was walking again and flipped myself out of bed in the middle of the night while I was sleeping. Finally, after ten or more years I have more acceptance of my injuries and realize I will not ever walk again, but just because I can't walk doesn't mean I can't live. I do live and make the best out of it.

I would get depressed from pain and my losses but thankfully I have a wonderful family and great support system in my life. I did learn to accept my new life and make the best of it.

I hear all the time people feel so bad for themselves because they need a surgery, or they hurt their back or something else. They don't realize how lucky they are to have something so minor happen to them. I always think at least there is a cure that can help them to be in less pain, for me there is nothing. I guess I am the wrong person to complain to. I had to become strong at a young age otherwise I wouldn't have made it this far.

Everyone Journey through life is important, and some our unfortunate to have more than others, and have it severely hard for a very long time. Don't ever give up! Stay positive and always remember the good you have in your life; it really does help to get you through your dark days.

Chapter Thirteen

So how do I feel about the person who hit us? I am often asked; I would be lying if I didn't say I am angry. I have been through pure hell and so much pain and suffering that I wouldn't wish on anyone.

Do I think of him often? No, I do not; I don't waste my energy on him. My energy needs to go on me, to give me the strength I need to live each day. But I have to say when I am stressing or having spasms that I can't bear, I do say a few Choice words.

When I hear my mother sharing our story at High Schools, Driving Schools or DUI/OUI recovery victim classes and talks about

"Life is about the Choices & Decisions we make." This is so true!

She shares that my father didn't choose to die and be in a coffin, he didn't choose to not see his children grow up and enjoy life.

My sister's didn't choose to grow up without a father and watch me suffer in so much pain. They didn't choose to witness the hardship, suffering, and hospital stays that I had to go through.

My mother didn't choose to lose her husband, to be a single parent. She didn't choose to watch me scream in pain, watching my bones curve my body and feeling helpless. She didn't choose to not be with her little girls and live in hospitals.

The man who hit us did choose to take Cocaine, and consume alcohol, he did make a choice to not have a designated driver and get behind a wheel. Yes, he didn't plan on killing anyone, but he did make a choice.

Life is about good choices and decisions and only we can make them. Our vehicle should not be used as a weapon to kill or injure someone. If you can't obey the rules of driving, then you shouldn't have a license.

We have to remember driving is a privilege.

Do I think our court system is for us victims? Sorry to say it is not. If you kill someone or paralyze someone like me, and have no chance of recovery, you should be sentenced to a maximum of twenty years in prison.

After serving many years, I believe their license should be taken away for a long time. If they do drive again, a breathalyzer should be required for several years after that.

Some of you may think this is too much to ask for, however, try living my life with all the pain, surgeries and procedures I endured for the last Twenty-six years, then tell me what you think.

I didn't get to go in front of a judge and ask for a second chance, I am a prisoner in my own body, I have a life sentence! My dad is in a coffin, he doesn't get to plead guilty and come back. If only it was that easy for victims.

What I don't get is why our system lets you plead guilty to a crime that they did commit and then they serve a low sentence after killing someone.

The man who hit us pleaded guilty, and gets a slap on the wrist sentence, of three to five years, this is a joke!

There was no sentence for killing my father; Doucette was only sentenced for severely injuring someone.

Our system allows you to get out on good behavior, so your sentenced time is even shorter.

They say there isn't enough room in prisons to keep prisoners. This is wrong, make room, find a way. It is so unfair to the people who passed away and for our loved ones to be without their family member. It is also unfair for people who have survived and now left paralyzed or with a TBI, or other injury that was life changing for them.

I will never be released from my pain and my father will never have a chance at life again. The best part is, we did nothing wrong, and our lives were forever changed with so much hardship and loss.

When you go through this type of tragedy, you have three choices; you can let it Define you, Destroy you or Strengthen you.

I choose to strengthen me; I can't give up and my family wouldn't allow this anyways. I was taught from the beginning that life must go on and we will survive and find new ways of doing everything.

My father wouldn't want us to give up on life because he is no longer here, we are determined to make the best life possible.

I am honored to carry my father's last name.

My father always said that I was in charge when he wasn't around, and I do take this seriously. I am determined to make him proud.

Yes, the laws of driving impaired should be changed, I know it will never come to a twenty-year sentence in prison, for our type of crash but you shouldn't be able to plead guilty. It should be a mandatory twenty-year prison term at least. This still isn't justice but at least it's better than three to five years.

We need to toughen up our laws so people make better choices and decisions. When they are released, they should have a stipend to pay monthly for medical expenses that they have caused or pay the victims family to help the person with medical needs and necessities. The needs our never ending and Health Insurance doesn't cover every need. So, guess what, it becomes our expense and if you can't afford it, oh well you suffer and must go without.

When our crash happened on Route 20, D. O. T. looked into fixing the corner on the Charlton/Oxford town line. Money was allotted, but when it was really looked at, they realized it was a much bigger project to do and the expense was huge. It was put on the books to do in fifteen to twenty years.

The money that was granted to fix Route 20 was now used to purchase barriers all down Route 20 instead. Yes, it helped in those areas, but it did nothing for the curve, also known as, "Dead Man's Curve", that has taken many other lives besides my father.

Years back, mom and I were asked by Chief Pervier of Charlton to go testify for the route 20 project. We were told that the project was taken off to be fixed because of the cost. We were in shock!

We testified to put the Route 20 project back on the books to be reconstructed. Thankfully the board heard my mom loud and clear of what this tragedy has brought to our family. The board voted all in favor to keep the reconstruction as scheduled. We were excited that Route 20 would still be on the books to be fixed in 2023.

In 2015, some guardrails were installed on the Charlton/Oxford town line on Route 20 to stop head on collisions. This should have happened when our crash took place, instead it took two more deaths to make it happen sooner.

What a shame, and how disappointing, yes there will still be crashes from impaired driving, these guardrails won't prevent crashes, but it will prevent head on collisions. The goal is to have concrete barriers in this area and is still scheduled to start in 2023.

When I seen the construction on Route 20 had begun, I have to say it made me happy to know that finally something was being done. We took my father's cross home that was on Route 20 for the past 18 years to clean it up. It was an emotional day for my mom when she brought the cross home, she was in tears, she felt like she was taking daddy home with her.

We painted the cross white and added new letters for our last name. We also put a sticker picture of my Mom's book, "A Mother's Journey," on it. It came out beautiful. The cross was five feet tall. It was huge. It was brought back to Route 20 and is now placed on top of the wall.

My mother was excited and thankful for the work being done by D. O. T. that she called the foremen up to bring the guys some pizza. She chose Papa Gino's because that was our last meal as a family together, before our car crash. When she went to pick up the pizza at Papa Gino's in Auburn, MA the manager was overwhelmed with the story behind it and donated the pizzas. One good deed turned into two great deeds of appreciation.

I am excited to say, it's the year of 2023. The construction that should have happened when our crash took place and fought for is finally happening on Route 20. It's only been a few months, a lot of clearing of trees and brush and now some new electrical poles our being placed. I can't wait to see in a few years when it is completed what it will look like.

In 2018 Mom and I were on our way to a High School presentation, it was a snowy day and we had to go by were our crash happened on Route 20. We were coming up Route 20 this time from Charlton and a huge tractor trailer was on the other side coming down and the trailer slid going around the curve in the snow and jack knifed into the guardrails.

Boy was that scary, thankfully the guardrails were in place because we could have been killed in the same spot of our crash. We definitely had our guardian angel with us.

Our family could of easily lost it after our crash in 1997. Thankfully my mother held us all together. We really didn't have a choice; she wouldn't let us think life was over. For me she made sure I discovered life in a different way. We learned together as a family how to enjoy life again and how to make fun times happen with so many memories to look back on.

When my sister's fought or weren't behaving she let them know, she always disciplined us using our father.

Mom would say,

"Your father would not be happy on how your acting" "Just because daddy isn't here with us, it doesn't mean he is not watching you".

When we did something good or accomplish an achievement my mother always says,

"How proud daddy and her are".

For the last twenty-six years my sisters and I receive a Christmas present in my father's memory from our mother. This is always one of our favorite gifts and it's the last gift we open each year.

For many years we all went to the cemetery with balloons writing a special message and hoping he would receive it. This was important to us especially when we were little because we felt like we were doing something for our father especially on his birthday or father's day. Writing our father, a little message or drawing him a picture meant the world to us. Now that we are older it doesn't happen as much, but I do believe it helped us with growing up and believing our father was with us.

Every Halloween my sister's, nieces and nephews, mom, and I go to the cemetery to decorate my father's stone. We all love it.

We place giant spiders on the front and back of his stone and black flowers in the two vases. The kids have fun, and they know their grandfather is buried there. We have done this for the last four years and now is a yearly family tradition.

One thing we all love is that on my father's gravestone there is a picture of him with my mother. We love to look at his picture, and see him, instead of the ground.

When I die, I will be placed near my father, and my mom will be on the other side of me. I will be with my parents, surrounded with love.

Am I afraid to die? I am not sure how to answer that.

I don't want to die, but I know when it happens my father will be waiting for me. I won't miss all my spasms and pain; I will be free and whole once again.

For now, I want to live, and do as much as I can to enjoy life to the fullest. I intend to leave a mark in this world!

Chapter Fourteen

My mother and I present our heartfelt story on impaired driving at schools and other forums. We leave are audience with a powerful message to never drive impaired in any way.

The first few years of presenting, we put the students in body jackets, body cast and, in a wheelchair. The students were asked how it felt? Many hated it and some in tears. They just couldn't imagine having to use one of these contraptions for a long period of time or possibly forever.

I spent years in some of these contraptions. My wheelchair is for life! The students can't imagine being myself, I always am told,

"I could never do this, and how do you do it?"

I don't have a choice. Someone that made a bad choice to drive intoxicated, and takes Cocaine put me in this position. I wish I could change it but I can't. It is what it is. I wouldn't wish my life on anyone.

When my mother talks to students and adults about all my losses it doesn't make me angry. I want to teach our young students and adults to make good choices. I don't want anyone to suffer the way I have. It's no picnic, my life is so many surgeries and doctor appointments.

I lived in a lot of pain! I screamed for years with so many spasms, my whole body was taken over by my severe dystonia and curved all my bones.

Now my muscle tone is throughout my body but mostly in my neck and now affecting my good arm. I still have spasms, but my baclofen pump and Botox helps to maintain it to a point where I can enjoy life some.

In-between it all, I try to find the good times. One thing I learned is that life is hard and if I want to be happy I have to find my own happiness. I try to always have something fun to do or something to look forward to.

During our presentation we talk about our crash, my father's last words "Oh My God" when we got hit by a pick-up truck. Myself fighting for every breath. My sisters were crying for my mother, my mom trapped in the car and injured. Burying my father, telling my sisters that daddy has died and myself so injured, survival guilt, meeting the man who crashed into us, and trying to heal and having the courage to go on with life.

It's difficult loosing a father he loved me unconditionally. He adopted me, out of love. My dad was so proud to give me his last name and I am honored to have it. I will always keep my father alive in my heart and let everyone know how special of a man he was.

He would be surprised by how my mother and I spread awareness about our crash and with our book, "A Mother's Journey Through Faith, Hope, and Courage. Our story is changing lives and shows how a life is changed in a quick second. High school and driving education programs have put our book in their learning curriculum. The feedback from students and adults has been heartwarming. The letters we receive privately are so touching, and students ask for help on their personal journey. Adults telling us we helped save their marriage by sharing our story. Some are no longer drinking alcohol and it has made them a better parent. Others now have a designated driver if they plan on consuming alcohol.

Parents are realizing that going out to eat and having several drinks and not having a designated driver can be dangerous.

Young children are asking my mom how to tell their parent they don't want to get in their parent's car after they were drinking alcohol. They don't want to have an accident and the possibility of them getting hurt and suffer the way I do. It's shocking to us but my mom and I realize we are helping people and we need to keep sharing our story to help spread awareness. I am hoping when students and adults leave our presentation that they never forget what they heard and saw.

My mother tries to have them Imagine being me, no more privacy, totally dependent on every need. They can no longer talk, walk or just put two feet on the ground again.

I can't use a cell phone, I don't have the air in my lungs to talk, I only have the use of one arm to do little things. I can't even itch myself, brush my teeth, my independence is gone. I am totally dependent on every need. This really makes the students think on what it could be like.

When they go to bed that night and they think of everything they heard and imagine being dependent on every need and want, it is devastating to them.

We have received messages from parents thanking us for this, because it really touched their child's heart.

I love at the end of presentations when the students or adults come talk to me. I love to arm wrestle and take pictures. They say thank you for sharing our story and tell me how strong I am. I just hope they never forget and always make good choices and decisions.

My mom and I had the honor of receiving four awards, Fox 25 "The Hometown Hero's", The Celtics "Hero's Among Us", The MIAA Wellness Partner of the Year Award, and the 2017 Charlton Old Home Day Humanitarian Award.

I have to say my favorite award is the Celtics "Hero's Among Us". The Celtics staff gave us a great day and it was so much fun watching the game and sharing our story in front of 22,000 people. My father would be so proud to know his face was put on the Arbitron. My dad loved sports and he always went to games. I know we made him proud.

We were also blessed with doing many podcast and TV interviews. We have met so many wonderful people in our journey.

I do wonder where I would be today if this crash didn't happen. Would I be married?

Have children?

What kind of job would I be doing?

So many questions, and no answers.

I will never know, it's something I must accept, and I can't dwell on. If I was to guess, I think I would have a trade, maybe an electrician. I would of loved to be married and have a family of my own. I can only dream and try to focus on what is today and only wonder what tomorrow will bring.

Just because someone is in a wheelchair or has a disability it doesn't make them any less of a person than you. Don't ever be afraid to approach me or others. I love to socialize and meet new people.

Don't let a disability or someone in a wheelchair scare you off. Be considerate if you see them struggling to get through a door, holding the door helps more than you realize and all I would say to you is thank you!

I did get a bad deal in life, but we also have feelings and wants just like you do. We want to be accepted and loved for who we are. We are human and if you give us a chance you might learn something from us that will make you a better and caring person. If you got to know me, I bet I would put a smile on your face.

My life may be hard, but I am thankful to be alive and I know I am making a difference in this life.

Are you making a difference, something to think about??

My sister's, nieces, nephew, mom and I
decorating my father's stone for halloween, 2023

If I Can Smile, I Can Live

Our Christmas gift in memory of our father, 2022

Mom and I receiving The Celtics Hero's Amongst Award, 2017

Chapter Fifteen

When my sisters, Katie, and Kimberly got engaged I was so happy for all of them. Planning their weddings was fun and very busy.

Katie was the first to get engaged and asked me to give her away since we lost our dad, I had a big smile, I am honored to give my little sister away. My father always said, "I was the one in charge when he was away", I have to say I helped my mother bring up my little sister's.

I made sure they knew who their father was, by having them watch home videos repeatedly. They got to know their father and his sense of humor and how he loved us all through these videos. Since my father is not here to give Katie away, I am so glad Katie chosen me to do this honor.

Tyler her fiancé asked me to be his best man. I had two very important roles to play. I took them very seriously. Our biggest worry was with me being in a wheelchair that I wouldn't run over Katies bridal gown.

The week finally came, my tux came in and mom had to do a lot of adjustments to my jacket including hemming the sleeves and hemming my pants. I was so excited I couldn't sleep for days before the wedding.

I had so much happening in one week. I was going to visit my old school, I had a doctor's appointment, two birthday parties for myself then a two-night sleepover at the Colonial Hotel where the wedding was.

With all the excitement I still couldn't sleep; I kept my mother up for days before the wedding. I got myself so worked up that I vomited, my oxygen level was in the high 80's, fever of 101 Degrees. I was nervous that I was going to be in the hospital and miss my sister's wedding. My mother got my temperature down and got me relaxed so I didn't have to go to the hospital. The next day I was good, still tired but I could not sleep.

My mother was so worried about sleeping at the hotel for the two nights because she knew I wouldn't sleep. This meant Lenny and her wouldn't get any sleep either. I didn't make any promises that I knew I couldn't keep. Well guess what, I stayed up all night talking, Lenny and mom were not too happy with me.

Lenny got so mad that he took me home at 6 am, I was so upset and had a few words for him. My mother didn't even stop him, I was shocked she let him bring me home. She was angry also, but I guess she had a right to be, it was her daughter's wedding day and I kept her up all night long.

Since Lenny brought me home, he had to take care of me. This included, putting me to bed, giving me my medicine, and bathing me. I knew I better behave and be nice because I wanted to go back to the wedding.

Lenny brought me back to the hotel for 2:00 PM, my mom got me dressed and Lenny put me in my chair.

Off I went with Lenny to go take pictures with the guys in the wedding party.

The time has come, I have two important roles to do! I am rolling my sister down the aisle, and I am best man. Did you know that meant I will receive two wedding gifts. I made sure they knew that.

I was given orders by my sister's. I couldn't take off with my motorized chair, I had to let Katie control it, I had to stay quiet during the ceremony! I chose to not use my head rest, that meant I had to try to hold my head up as best as I could. These were hard task for me since I don't like to listen.

The wedding is starting; everyone is lined up ready to go in. The grandparents, and parents are being escorted to their seats.

The music changes, now the bridesmaids are all going in one by one. Kimberly, the maid of honor is in front of me, she takes me and puts me in the back of the aisle and tells me to wait for Katie and not to move. She kissed me and walked down the aisle.

I did everything I was told; I didn't move. The music changes once again, Katie comes over to me, rubs my head and said,

"Are you ready"? I smiled.

She took control of my chair, my hand over hers and I escorted her down the aisle with pride. She was so beautiful.

When she got to the end of the isle where Tyler was standing, my mother came over and the minister asked,

"Who gives Katie away?" and my mother said, "We do" and then put me next to Tyler since I was one of the best mans.

The ceremony started, but I must confess, I nodded off, I was so tired. I was awakened by one of the groomsmen. Before I knew it, my baby sister was married and now we were taking pictures. Soon the fun part will begin with the reception.

The wedding party was all introduced and walked to their seats. When it was time for me to be introduced my sister Kimberly took my tray off, and she sat on my lap while driving us into the hall. It was so exciting!

Since I was the best man, I gave a speech using my I-Pad. This is what I said:

Katie Bear and Ty Ty,

Congratulations:

Tyler now that you are married let me give you the scoop on my little sister! I hope you know you won't be getting your way any longer, with Katie's beauty and contagious smile she will always win you over! She can be a little bit stubborn at times, however, she didn't get that from me! ! Just give her a smile and do what she wants. Remember, a happy wife makes a happy home! When you come home at the end of the week just hand Katie all your hard-working money. Katie will handle everything from now on. When Katie takes me to buy my new iPad. I will come to thank you, for your generous gift!

Katie, you definitely caught the best fish of Lake Chaubunagungomaug.

Our father would have been proud to call Tyler his son in law. I am honored to have Tyler as my brother from another mother. Katie, you are not just beautiful on the outside but the inside where it matters the most. You both have been blessed to have found each other!

The best advice I can give you is what our father always said. "Always kiss each other goodnight" and "Never go to bed angry". I will always be here for the both of you if you ever need to vent. My fee is only $100 dollars an hour! Congratulations and the best of luck always!

Everyone seemed to love my speech, so many people laughing. Now I had one more honor to do then I could enjoy the party and my date.

After the meal we started with the dancing, now the hardest dance of all was the father and daughter dance. Since my father passed away, Katie made a video of her and our father dancing. She used home video's from when she was three-year-old and she added pictures of them two, while my father was singing "Beautiful in my Eyes".

It was so touching and was a beautiful tribute to our father. Katie danced to the video playing on two TV screens with the special men in her life, and I had the honor of starting the dance with her.

There were a lot of tears shed remembering our father, but no one could ever replace the special father we had.

We had a great wedding day and a party after the wedding. Cheryl, my little sister's mother decided to keep me in her hotel room for that night to give my mom a break.

Guess what? even after having a few drinks and one shot I still didn't sleep. Cheryl and my sister were very tired the next day and I was ready to go. I am still trying to figure out where all this energy came from, since I lacked so much sleep this week.

I have to say once I arrived home and got in my own bed I slept for hours, and I even stayed home the next day and enjoyed sleeping.

My mother said, "Never again will she do this, I will have my own hotel room next to hers". If I choose to stay up it's my loss not hers. I did apologize, my mother knows I can't control all the excitement I have in my life. It's just the way my body handles it. Thank God my mom is not use of a lot of sleep.

God and my father gave her the strength she needed to get through the day. We all had a great day, and I am happy to say I have gained a brother-in-law and his wonderful family.

When Kimberly got engaged to Kyle, Kim said,

"Since you did a great job with Katie, I would like you to walk me down the aisle."

I was so excited, because it meant the world to me. I know my father was looking down and was happy they were having me do this honor.

This time I knew what to expect. I promised Kimberly, I would behave and not run over her dress, smiling.

She just said, "You better not". I love kidding my sister!

So much wedding planning and fun times were ahead. My biggest worry was I had to sleep at night, and I couldn't keep my mother awake again.

A week before the wedding, I was admitted to the hospital, I was having seizures. Mom and I were so worried about the wedding, I didn't want to miss it, and mom never leaves me in a hospital, unless it is an emergency. It was nerve wracking. I was discharged four days before the wedding. Thankfully I knew I could be at the wedding and give my sister away.

Mom decided I would not stay at the Chocksett Inn, the night before the wedding. We all needed to sleep, and with me just getting out of the hospital, I needed to be in my own bed to play it safe for the wedding day. I wasn't too happy about it, but there was nothing I could do. My PCA Claire, took me to the restaurant, the night before the wedding so I could be with everyone for the meal and gathering. Claire slept at my house that night and in the morning, she bathed me, got me dressed in my tuxedo and then brought me to the hotel for the wedding.

It was very busy when I arrived, all the bridesmaid's and bride were getting their hair done and everyone was so excited. Lenny took me so I could be with the guys, mom came after and made sure my jacket was all set on me.

The time has come, all the guest our arriving, we our all waiting outside to enter the gazebo area. Kyle goes to take his place, the music has started, the grandparents and parents walk down the aisle, then the bridesmaid's and flower girl.

Katie brought me to my position for Kimberly. Now the maid of honor, Katie, walks down the aisle.

The music changes, and Kimberly walks over to me, she gives me a kiss and puts her hand on my controller to drive my chair, I put my hand on top of hers, I gave her a big smile and we rolled down the aisle. Kimberly looking so beautiful holding her train, so I don't run over it.

We arrived at the end of the aisle where Kyle was standing, my mother came over and the minister asked,

"Who gives Kimberly away?" My mother said, "We do" and then put me in line with the other ushers.

I was exhausted and the heat was getting to me, I was having a seizure during the ceremony. My mother watching closely, thankfully I was okay. Mom said she was so worried; she was thankful that we got through the ceremony. I was given a cold drink and cold towel which helped.

Kimberly and Kyle were now married, I had another brother-in-law. I was excited!

We took plenty of pictures then we were announced into the wedding. I rolled in with my cousin LeeAnna, we had shades on and pretended we were driving, it was a cute little skit we did, Driving Dirty, everyone looked so beautiful especially my sister Kimberly.

Since my father couldn't be here, I wrote a speech for Kimberly and Kyle on my I-pad.

This is what I said:

Kimberly and Kyle,

Kyle, I have to tell you our father would have loved you! He would have been proud to call you his son- n- law you have so many great qualities like our father. I couldn't have picked a better person for my baby sister.

Kyle, today I handed you over the middle child. This beautiful sister of mine may be a little bit short, but does she have spunk, and will tell you just the way it is. So, get ready, all I can suggest is take a deep breath, put some ear plugs in, wait until she's done, then give her a twisted tea to calm her down. Make sure it's cold and not hot.

If you really want to be smart hand over a little cash, this might put a little smile on her face because she loves to go shopping.

Kimberly happens to be very intelligent; I would say she gets her brains from her father and from me of course. I taught her many things especially love and kindness. Kimberly, I know you will carry these traits over now to your husband and to my future nieces and nephews. You have a heart of gold, I worked very hard on these traits, and I am proud to call you, my sister.

Kyle if you ever need advice on how to handle Kimberly, I will always be here, us brothers need to stick together. I'm only one phone call away, don't forget to bring the Jack Daniels and coke, I will need it.

Kimberly, you have married a fireman that loves to put out hot flames. You will be the hottest flame he ever had to conquer. One that Kyle will never be able to put out. Kyle, please take this spatula, see how it says Mr. Right, well sorry to say those days are over, now that you are married. Hand it over to your beautiful bride, now it's Mrs. Always Right.

Kyle, of all the guy's Kimberly could have chosen she chosen another Kyle. Our name is a strong name we are determined individuals to keep going and to never give up. So, make me proud and always be there for my baby sister.

The best advice I could give you both, is don't stay mad, say your peace and get over it, and always kiss each other good night.

Best of luck to the both of you, and many happy years together for the rest of your lives.

Kimberly had a father's dance, she played Beautiful in my eyes, that her father had sang. She danced with her husband with a video playing in the background of her and her daddy slow dancing. It was an emotional memory for so many.

Now one more wedding to go, my sister Breanna.

She is in her last year of college. So, I still have some time before that happens.

I had the honor of giving my sister Katie away at her wedding, 2015

My sister and I being introduced at Katie's wedding, 2015

I had the honor of giving my sister Kimberly away at her wedding, 2018

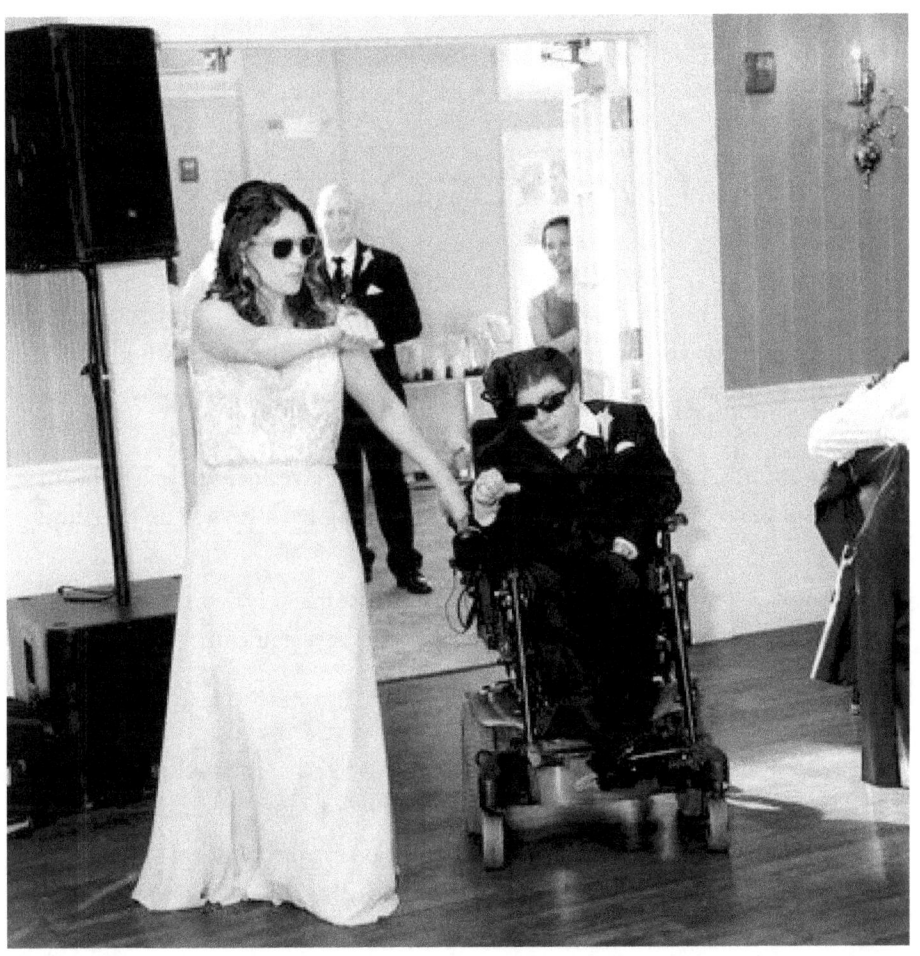

My cousin LeeAnna and I being introduced at Kim's wedding, 2018

Chapter Sixteen

Hopefully you will never be in a situation like me. Whether it's a crash, accident, sickness, sport injury or even born this way, it doesn't matter how it happened, we are paralyzed.

I want to share some helpful ideas that I have learned over the past twenty-six years of having a life of care and finding new ways to do everything I do.

I know it's a hard thing to accept, but in some way, you must come to terms with it in order to go on and live life the best you can.

Care at home,

Always use bed pads, one you can wash or throwaways. I use the ones you wash, but I always have the blue chucks throw aways in stock, this is good for traveling or if I feel like vomiting. Mass Health does cover this for me.

I use a hospital bed; a bed is covered by Mass Health but don't be surprised if you get a used one. If you are paralyzed and you can't put your feet on the floor, you will get a cranked bed to go up or down. You will get a controller to move your upper body, and legs up or down. Mass Health does not care about the caregivers; it is just what the patient needs are. This makes it hard for the caregivers, especially if they our tall or have a bad back. I use bed risers to make my bed higher and it is much easier for my caregivers.

If you cannot move in bed, you are best to purchase an alternating air mattress. Sad to say Insurance doesn't cover this unless you have a stage three bedsore. I buy mine on Amazon, and its affordable. The air mattress tends to last a couple of years then it's time for a new one. You need to adjust to it but with all the pillows I use its perfect for me. I do not have to worry about bedsores, this is very important. My skin tends to break down easy.

I use several pillows for comfort, I am a side sleeper, but because of my spasms I have been sleeping on my back which I hate, but I am adjusting to it. I can no longer sleep on my right side.

I like a thick pillow under my head, a thick pillow on the left side of my head, a thin pillow to go in-between my legs for comfort. We also put a thick pillow near the thin pillow to hold my leg in place. I also use a wedge for my back to help keep me on my side. I can't go much on my side but just a little. They make smaller wedges now, which is nice. We buy the pillows and wedge. Insurance should cover the wedge with a prescription.

I am in a brief, yes, I hate it, but I don't have a choice. The brand I use is Depends. I also use men guards to help me not go through the brief so much. It seems no matter what we do, almost every night I go through the brief and wet my pads and t-shirt. Yes, it's a lot of wash, but again it is what it is. I didn't like a catheter, it's a pain. Mass Health does cover my briefs.

I use a tray to eat in bed, my tray holds my drink. It's best to use a straw and a cup with a cover. I purchase this item. Mass health will cover a Bed table that is used in hospitals. Nowadays I tend to eat more while in my wheelchair.

I use a barrier-free lift; it's the best. This lift is used to get me in and out of my chair several times each day. I have tracking on the ceiling in my bedroom that goes to my bed and shower. It is very easy for your caregiver to use. You can purchase a free barrier stand if you don't want a track in your ceiling.

You can also purchase a mobile lift that you could use for a pool, if you have a pool pole with the attachment to hold the Barrier Free Lift.

You would need tracking or a Free Barrier Stand above your hot tub to use if your hot tub is inside like mine.

You will need to have a sling for everyday use, and one for a shower, pool or hot tub.

Sad to say this lift is not covered by Mass Health but the sling may be if you use a Hoyer sling and have a Hoyer lift at home.

I have a walk-in shower, with a Shower Gurney with elevating headrest that I lay down on. I love it. We use two shower heads; one I can hold, or my caregiver can rinse me off. The other shower head keeps me warm with constant running water. I love the handheld shower because I enjoy getting my caregiver all soaked.

Trying to fight muscle tone? This is a huge challenge, I tend to squeeze a ball, stretch my arm more often. I am trying Botox injections now. If I am having spasms in my legs, I immediately go to bed, I am laid flat in bed, with a pillow in-between my legs. I take extra medicine to help calm me down and my mother will put relaxing music on for me.

If it's nighttime, my sound machine will be put on, which I love. This will tend to help me relax, and my mom leaves the room, so I have no distraction.

If I am sweating, I will have a cold face cloth, water and a folded flat sheet, that is put over my pink pad, that I lay on, to help me be cooler and it helps me not to sweat so much.

I have special eating utensils, I have plates that have sides on them, I also have a bowl that helps me when I try to feed myself. There is lots of choices for silverware, plates and bowls or other accessories that you may need. Insurance may pay for this, but we tend to buy it.

I use an Apple I-pad, it's my favorite. My program I use is the Prologuo2Go from Apple, I highly recommend it. It does everything you need it to do. Mass Health didn't cover this for me. I also use a stand to hold my I-pad on my tray. I purchase my I-Pad holder from RJ – Cooper. This sight has many different items for many disabilities, you will be amazed!

I have a push wheelchair, that I use, to go visit family. My motorized chair is too hard, because it is heavy and harder to move to make corners. Most houses our not accessible for me.

I purchase ramps to get up the couple stairs they may have. Ramps our not covered by Mass Health.

I have a motorized wheelchair that has a special custom head rest, air cushion for my seating and if you have a scoliosis problem you may need a molded back cushion to fit your needs.

I have moveable leg rest and calf support for my legs and a foot-strap holder for one of my feet. You will need a wheelchair company to assist in getting you a wheelchair. You need a prescription from your primary doctor and a Physical Therapist. I currently use National Seating for my wheelchair company.

My chair has a tilt mode, I can't do a recline mode, I have lights for night time, a backup mirror and my chair rises twelve inches.

It's a new world to be higher in my chair. I can even go to a bar now and sit at the bar like everyone else does. I can be in a conversation and be eye level with everyone. I can reach items now and put my plate and cup in the sink. This is huge for me since I haven't been able to do this in twenty years. These are things everyone takes for granted until you can no longer do it.

What I can't believe is my insurance wouldn't cover it. It wasn't a medical necessity. My hardware let go in my neck, so my neck is down a lot, I have seizures, and mv vision is affected by straining my eyes to look up at people. Having the height to rise to everyone's level helps my vision to not strain. It has opened my world up a little more. I will self-pay for the elevation rising and the backup mirror. Everyone is different in their needs, but all these items on my chair are a necessity for me.

Transportation – I purchased a Kneel van, we love it, and it makes life much easier to have your own vehicle. Vans our not covered by insurance. I use a back entry; my driver manually puts down the lift, I drive right in the van, then my wheels our fastened down. I have a bucket seat on each side of me, it's perfect if we have more than two passengers. I love it when I have people sit on the side of me.

This is my fourth van, and I have to say, I love the Honda Odyssey the best.

If you don't own or have access to a handicap vehicle, your medical plan should pay for transportation back and forth from your medical appointments. This is all that insurance will cover for transportation if you live at home.

We built a customhouse; we enlarged all our doors, hallways, and stairs. I have my ramp in the garage, so I never have to worry about the snow or it being slippery.

I have a lift for the stairs, that I drive my wheelchair on to. This stair lift brings me in the cellar. We have a walkout basement with cement ramps.

My house is all open, and the island in the kitchen is placed where I can drive around it. It's perfect for me and I can go wherever I want.

Years ago, I was able to use a Free stander, this is good if you're trying to strengthen your legs. Insurance should cover this.

The Action Track Chair – lets you go on rough terrain, beaches, or in the snow, you can even purchase a plow for the snow. This is a motorized track chair. It can even go up in a stand position. I think it is now approved for veterans to help pay for it. You would have to investigate it. It is life changing if you like the woods, hunting or other hobbies. Actiontrackchair. com

Hoyt running chair- someone pushes this chair. It is great for the beach, running, rough terrain, or biking. It comes in Fat tires and road tires. It also comes apart for travel and has an attachment you can purchase to be pulled with a bike.

I use travel pillows and a neck travel pillow to help keep me comfortable in the Action Track and Running chairs. It is life changing and lets you enjoy life more.

Contact is: Hoytrunningchairs. com

Personal Care Attendants our very hard to find. Most don't give notices when they decide to leave. I was lucky to have all my sisters' work for me, now they are all grown up and now it's all new people. I have been lucky with a few that stayed for a few years. This will always be a challenge, sad to say.

The best advice I can give you is to try to make the best of it, focus on the good you have and what you can do. Don't dwell on your losses; find new ways of doing things.

At times you need to be creative to make it work, other times it takes phone calls to people that may have experience in finding ways to make it happen. Specialty departments at hospitals, PT, OT, wheelchair businesses, and research on Google could help you out.

If you are a parent, let your child/adult live, don't treat them any different. They are not babies; if they still have their mind let them do their dreams, find a way. Let them live life to the fullest.

Always be honest and let them help make decisions for themselves. Get them involved with different things to do, get creative, don't just let them sit there and think there isn't anything they can do.

Yes, it is work for you caregivers or parents but when you see your child or love one light up, it will mean the world to you.

Always remember, "Life is for the living", Be that Inspiration and remember there is always someone that has it worse than you! Giving Up is Not an Option!

Chapter Seventeen

Wow, this Covid pandemic changed my life totally. I was in Florida with Lenny and mom when it all started. We had to drive home and hotels were closed, even some convenient stores were not open. We took Route 95, which was the fastest way. Our navigation said an eighteen-hour drive. Mom made us food and plenty of snacks to have just in case. We stopped often, so Lenny and mom could stretch, driving this distance is extremely hard on all of us.

I started to have it hard after ten hours, Lenny would boost me in my wheelchair every time we stopped, and I took extra meds to help me with any pain I was in. Our dog Allie was driving with Lenny in his truck, Allie overall did great she got to stretch her legs often at each stop.

The funniest part of driving home was when mom needed to use a bathroom and we couldn't find one that was open to the public.

I kept saying "Use one of my diapers," but she said, "No."

We had a bucket in our van so mom decided she would pee in that, it was hilarious. If you know my mom, you know she was laughing and of course she made a mess. Lenny was in shock, she was peeing in a bucket in the back of the van, at least she was inside the van and not outside. After that eventful moment we were back on the road, all refreshed and wide awake from laughing so much.

We arrived at 2 am in the morning and we couldn't get to bed fast enough. We had so much stuff to take out of the van just to get me out.

Immediately my electric bed was turned on and as soon as it was ready, mom put me in it. I had to say it felt so good to be in bed and out of my chair.

It feels good to be home, but I love going to Florida. I love the sunshine and making new memories. We all dread the long ride home but we are glad we made it home safely.

I couldn't wait to see my family but due to Covid we couldn't, we all missed the kids, so it was hard not to be able to see them.

Thankfully the weather wasn't too cold in April, so my sisters would come over and we would stay outside and from a distance see the kids. My nieces and nephew were young, so they didn't understand but it worked out.

My day program at the Center of Hope was closed, everything shut down, life was extremely different. Everywhere we went we had to wear a mask. I didn't go to stores or places for a long while, I tried to stay safe and not get the virus. After a while we all adjusted to the new way of living and being careful to not get others sick. We stayed away from everyone, even with a bit of a cough. I think it sound better.

Life for me really changed drastically, I no longer had a day program, my sport running races with Mike was no longer, all speaking events and craft fairs were cancelled.

Thank God I had my art, I could still paint to pass my time. As time went on, I definitely changed as a person, I missed being with people and doing all of my activities. Life was surely different; I didn't like it.

As time went on I found myself not as motivated, all of a sudden days definitely lasted longer. Thankfully mom had the children to babysit while my sisters worked. It helped to have company but I still found my days to be long. I only had a couple PCA's and at times just Lenny and mom cause if anyone was sick, they didn't come in.

I found my body was stressing so much, I had so many more spasms and I really didn't know why. Mom took me to several doctors; one was to check my spine to make sure it was holding from removing my hardware six years ago. I was told my spine was solid and that it couldn't be that causing my pain.

My hip was checked, it was all good. I was given some new meds, and it did nothing for me. I was in severe pain four to five days a week; my spasms would last for several hours. It was extremely hard for me.

My body was getting worse with my muscle tone curving my body more. I found my attitude was very different and depressing. I formed habits I didn't have, like talking while I was eating which made me choke, I was to stressed to use my I-pad, painting went from painting almost every day to only two or three times a week, I could no longer drive my track chair. I was crashing more with my motorized chair, my muscle tone know going in my one good arm, and my right leg crossing over to my left leg.

Mom was in tears often because she couldn't take me in all this pain. It also changed her as a person.

She said it felt like she was going back to the times when our crash first happened. Watching me in so much pain was making her anxious.

She would often give me extra meds, put me to bed, place me on my back, put music on and put a sound machine on with stars to try to help me to relax. She would leave the room; she needed a break. It affected us both and changed us both mentally and physically.

Mom would also, rock me while I was in bed on my side, and massage my body, I even talked her into given me marijuana drops under my tongue. We tried marijuana creams, marijuana cookies or gummies but nothing would work for me.

Mom called my doctor to increase my baclofen pump, mom told the doctor they couldn't find anything medically wrong with me, so it was okay to do.

Luckily my doctor let me come in the next day and my Baclofen pump was programmed to have an increase daily and a bolus feed everyday at four O'clock.

In no time my spasms started to decrease, I was doing great for three weeks. I found myself much happier, and now my mom was trying so hard to break my bad habits that I took on for the last year.

It was so tough, and mom wasn't easy on me, she didn't baby me any longer. She really wanted the old Kyle back and needed it badly. She kept telling me it was tough love again; I need to get back to my old ways and I had to stop being lazy and try.

I know she is correct but now I am not as ambitious, my body is in more pain because I curved more, its even harder for me than what it was.

One thing about my mom is that she doesn't give up, when she is determined she will do whatever it takes to make these changes.

Christmas came and we were very busy with family gatherings, mom was doing a lot of cooking and baking to give our family a great day. Everyone came down and we had a great day with plenty of presents and great food.

One of my PCA's was out sick for a week so thankfully Lenny and mom took care of me.

Mom or Lenny would be giving me my meds, and getting me ready for the day. I found myself very different, I was exhausted, weak, and my eyes were fluttering a lot.

Mom and Lenny kept asking me why are you so tired? Do you feel different? Mom asking me if I felt like I was having a seizure? My eyes were fluttering a lot.

Come late afternoon I would be more awake each day.

Bedtime would come and my night meds would be given again. Sadly it would sedate me and I would fall asleep fast. Mom couldn't figure out why, it made no sense.

Come to find out someone was taking my spasm medicine. Lenny, mom, my sisters and I were so hurt and saddened when we found out who it was. I just can't believe this person watched me suffer so badly and didn't care.

This person will never realize how badly my body was affected. In February, 2022 I was hospitalized for a twisted bowel, the doctors could no longer get a NG tube in me, I had to go to the OR to have it put in. Going to the OR to put in a NG tube is serious, if you aspirate it could be fatal. Thank god I only aspirated a little and I was good. I was told all my insides were swollen from all the stress my body was put under. I need to try to stay calm and stay stress free.

I have found my life so different and it has given me anxiety and at times I am also hitting myself in my head. I do not know why I do this it just happens.

My eating has improved some with not talking as much, I drove my track chair again, and I am still working on my other behaviors that I have gotten.

My muscle tone is in my good arm, neck and both legs, this has worsened because of my anxiety now. I have a lot to get through and I am working on improving my life again.

If I Can Smile, I Can Live

This person said they loved me, but how could you love me by taking my medicine and watching me suffer every night or day you were with me? You have made my life so much harder than it already was. I will get my life back in time, if my muscle tone allows me to, and hopefully I will get more motivated again.

I was extremely happy that Covid restrictions were lifted. Mom was always telling me my hair was turning gray.

I said, let's color it!

She said, "That's a great idea, we could put some blonde highlights in".

I was excited because I knew she would take me to Mane Creations. Mom been going to this salon since she was nineteen years old.

Mom called and asked Steven if he could color my hair. He said yes with no hesitation. Mom said it will be a challenge, but Steven said he would figure it out as it came and made me an appointment.

I was very excited knowing I would be going to the salon and to have a different look. I would also get to see Maria, the owner of Mane creations.

The day has arrived, I get to experience having my hair done. Steven helped my mom to get me inside the salon. I was greeted by Maria and received my hug and kiss on my cheek, this always brings a smile to my face.

Steven moved his salon chair so I could be placed in front of his mirror and then put a black cape on me. Mom raised my chair up higher to make it easier for him.

We talked about what I wanted done and about the color. Once we decided on the blonde highlights Steven went and mixed my color. He came back and explained he would put the dye in my hair and then placed a hair cap on me for an hour. I wanted the whole experience.

Then it was time to rinse my hair and wash it. Mom moved my motorized wheelchair and tilted it way back on the side of the sink. Steven held the water sprayer to rinse my hair and mom held a big trash bucket so the water could go in there.

We made it work, and it felt so good.

It was time for my haircut then a blow dry. I asked Steven to put gel in my hair, and he did happily.

I loved my new look, and I was so happy to experience having my hair done. It was a challenge to figure it out, but Steven, Maria and mom made it work for me.

I always look forward to going every three to four months and now Steven uses a cap on me and pulls the hair through the little holes. This way some of my hair is mixed with the blonde.

I get many compliments on my new look. I am thankful to Maria and Steven for taking the time and figuring out the best way to color, wash and cut my hair while dealing with my wheelchair. They do it with a smile and I know they care about me. They always make sure I am very happy before I leave, and I always get a nice hug and kiss goodbye from Maria. I am a lucky guy!

Mike and I love to be back running our races. Mom and I are back to vending and sharing our story to High Schools or wherever else we are asked to go.

I love meeting new people especially the pretty ladies. It doesn't look like I will ever have a day program again, the lists for one-to-ones our extremely long. People just don't want these kinds of jobs any longer, the salary needs to be raised.

I do miss my program at the Center of Hope, but it's been three years since I have been, and I know a lot of the people aren't there any longer. I hope soon I will be able to go back.

Thankfully my mom keeps me busy, we go for walks, we paint, have family over and babysit my nieces and nephews, doctors appointments, vending and of course shopping. Luckily in the winter we always go to Florida, that is always so much fun.

My life will come back to the way it was in time. It is work in progress, I will keep fighting all my battles and live the best possible life I can. I will never give up, I love life!

Chapter Eighteen

If I could go back to life at ten years old and do anything I would buy a Dino BMX Bike w/peg. I loved to do jumps and I really wanted to learn stunts with my bike. I know I would still be in Karate and playing my sports. I had so many things I loved to do.

I liked a girl back then and I would of most likely asked her out.

If I could change one thing, I wish I would have said no to my father to go shopping the day our crash happened. Yes, this does haunt me, but I do realize it's not my fault.

Yes, my life is different, but do I enjoy life? Yes, I do. I love to hang out with my family and love to visit with friends.

I love my sport with Team Unstoppable and love riding on rough terrain and all the amazing races Mike and I do together.

I enjoy playing games, listening to James Taylor, Beatles, Billy Joel, and especially the music that my father sang. I would love to meet Sophia Vergara, she is gorgeous and so funny! I would also love to meet Michael Jordan.

I had the pleasure of meeting Michael Jackson with my parents in Florida before our crash. I met James Taylor and went to his concert, Mike Tyson in Las Vegas, Tony Atlas at a wrestling event, Celtics players while being honored, Terry O"Reilly, Rick Middleton from the Boston Bruins, and Julian Edelman at best buddies.

I loved picking on my baby sister. When my sister Breanna was little, I would ask her to play hide n seek and she would always say yes. She would go hide, and I would never go find her. She would get so mad at me. We would love to scare her mother, Cheryl. Breanna would go hide in my closet, then I would press my horn on my wheelchair or try to be loud to have her mother come in my bedroom. Cheryl would come in, then Breanna would open the closet door and scare her. We always scared her so good.

One afternoon, a Home Depot floor man was at my house putting in a floor. Mom just purchased me a water gun that could shoot far, my mother filled it up for me, but she had no idea what I was doing.

Every time the floor man would walk in and out of my house, I would shoot him with my water gun. It was hilarious, he never said a word. Mom caught on after I already did it multiple of times. I laughed so much.

Another time I scared the heck out of David Nolin. We were having a fire at my house, and I was toasting a marshmallow, and I flung the long stick back and when it came forward it went high in the air on fire and attached to my house on the vinyl siding.

It stuck to my house, and it was on fire. David had to move so fast and get the hose and spray down where it was burning.

Another time with David we were out Roller skating and David was pushing me in my manual wheelchair, and suddenly, a little boy came flying in front of my wheelchair and fell down, there was nothing David could do, we were going at a fast speed, and we ended up running him over.

Thankfully the little boy was okay, but David never took me Roller skating again. Other than that, we had so much fun going round and round with the music playing and being with all the other roller-skaters.

One day Lenny, mom and I were in a waiting room at Children's Hospital. Lenny was on his phone, and I moved my motorized wheelchair and somehow, I got hooked to his chair.

Lenny was yelling at me to stop, and I kept going.

Lenny was being dragged in his chair with me across the room until I stopped!

If I Can Smile, I Can Live

I scared the heck out of him, if you could have only seen his face. Mom and I were laughing hysterically; after the shock of it all, Lenny was laughing also.

I have to say one of my favorite PCA's was Dan Healey, he worked for me every Saturday from 12 to 6 pm. We had a lot of fun together; he brought me everywhere and treated me like one of the guys. We have done so many things and made so many memories that made us laugh hysterically. We always played Mario 64 – Nintendo, we would go to parks and trails for walks, restaurants, museums, aquariums, libraries, strip joints, cigar stores, whatever I wanted we did even if he didn't want to do it, he did it to make me happy.

Dan always did whatever he could to make me laugh, he would always play up his frustration especially when I would go driving in an unkept field at Old Sturbridge Village.

Now my wheels our stuck and Dan would have to go find help to get me out of the field. We would love to go to the "Mekong Market" a Chinese grocery story and just walk the isle and laugh at the food we knew nothing about. We would purchase things like, aged eggs, crickets and fermented noodles then go back to the house and try to eat them. Of course, we both would gag trying to get a bite down.

We would also drive around and pick a restaurant out that we knew nothing about. Each of us would pick something off the menu for each other to eat. This was always interesting, sometimes we liked it other times we threw it away.

We would love to go to Friendly's and order the fifteen-scoop sundae. Dan and I pretended that it was a food challenge and we hyped each other up so we would eat the whole sundae. This always got Dan sick because he ate too much, we could never finish it.

Dan would even take care of me if I was sick. One day he brought me home and put me to bed, and I happen to projectile vomit. It went everywhere; even the floor. I was totally covered in vomit. Dan was trying to clean me up, but the poor guy couldn't take the smell, he went running in the bathroom and he puked too. Mom came home and she laughed hysterically.

When my days with Dan came to an end after ten years, I was saddened to lose him, but happy to say he married my cousin LeeAnna, and I was proud to be in their wedding. So happy Dan is part of my family!

My favorite one to one at the Center of Hope was Ben Doyen, I had him for many years, we shared many fun times together and many conversations about life and helped me on my bad days. He converted all my home videos to DVD's which took about a year to do. This was special to me because this was my life pretty much before our crash. Those videos contained many memories of my father.

Ben was very smart in video production and new the computer very well. He helped me with my I-pad and made my mom a video to do her presentations. We made some fun videos with Mike DiDonato at Southbridge Tool, and I would love when Ben took me there to visit.

I loved to go to Book's N Beans in Southbridge, but that has closed now. I have many memories going there and meeting friends and having a special drink that I made up called the Kyle Special. It even made the menu, it contained French vanilla coffee, cream, sugar, shot of hazelnut, coconut, green apple and lemon. It looked like a green swamp, but I would order it daily and drink it all. Ben finally broke down and tried it, but he said it was as gross as it sounds.

Ben and I would also sell my mom's baked goods to all the people at the Center of Hope on Fridays. Everyone went crazy for her home-made devil dogs with real cream, peanut butter fudge, zucchini and banana bread, cookies, and cupcakes. It was fun selling the baked goods, and all the profits went towards our fundraising that we do every year for the holidays

Ben and I would love to walk in the cemeteries and read the old gravestones. We would go to the library and study the Egyptian Greeks once a week or anything else I was interested in. Anywhere we would go, we always found people to talk to. We had a lot of fun together, sadly for me, Ben got a promotion at work, and I lost my friend my one to one.

Since then, my time at the Center of Hope was never the same again. I went through several one to ones after that, but it was all so different, some were good, but others were just lazy, and it wasn't as fun anymore. Then

If I Can Smile, I Can Live

the pandemic happened and even now that it is over, I still don't have a day program.

Since mom and I love fundraising mom had a crazy idea of putting me in jail to raise money for my day program at the Center of Hope.

We asked Mike DiDonato to be part of it and he immediately said yes. Boy did we have fun. We got pulled over by the police in Southbridge, Mass, we were handcuffed, fingerprinted, and even had mug shots taken. We were placed in a jail cell dressed in black n white prison outfit to look real.

Mike and I made so many funny videos, we had a great time playing this all out. Mom filmed all the scenes and then we made a video out of it and posted it to Facebook asking for donations to get Mike and I out of jail as soon as possible.

Within two days we raised a little over two thousand dollars. We were excited that people donated and helped my day program.

My biggest compliment I receive, is that people love my blue eyes.

My family tends to always run their fingers through my thick hair.

My favorite color is blue, because it makes my blue eyes pop.

Twenty percent or more of my time spent each day is on my I-pad, I love my computer and watching You Tube. I really love magic and funny videos.

I don't tend to really watch a lot of TV unless I am in bed. If I am going to watch it, I tend to love game shows, America got Talent, Baywatch, Friends, you tube videos of acrylic artist or Bob Ross. I never use to watch artist painting until I became interested in painting myself. I learned a lot from you tube artist and especially Bob Ross.

So how did I discover painting? It all started on Thanksgiving Day several years ago.

I was at my brother-in-law Tyler's parents house, his cousin Page, brought a craft for us to make with dough, I was given some dough and Tyler asked me,

"What do you want to make?"

I said, "my Hoyt running chair."

Tyler carved out my running chair for me. The dough would eventually get hard and then I could paint it.

I took it home and I was supposed to paint it, but it sat for about two years.

One day my sister Katie came over and said,

"Kyle, you never painted your running chair, do you want to paint it?"

I immediately said yes.

Katie yelled to my mom asking, "Do we have any paint in the house?"

Mom said, "No."

Katie said, "Can we order some from Amazon?"

Mom, said "Yes, you can."

Katie and I went on Amazon.com looking at paint, then I saw rollers, canvas, brushes and I wanted it all.

Katie yelled to mom asking, "Kyle wants canvas, rollers, brushes and paints, can he get them?"

Mom said, "Yes, that is fine."

So, we ordered it all and waited for it to come in. It came in, Katie came over and I started to paint. My paintings were beautiful, mom and Katie were in shock.

At that time mom and I were fundraising for the holidays to give back to the community, mom bakes and sells her baked goods, and we collect bottles and cans.

Mom said to me, "Kyle, would you like to see if we can sell these paintings for $10.00, and put it towards our fundraising efforts.

I said, "Yes".

Mom made a video of my paintings and put it on her Facebook page, A Mother's Journey, and they sold immediately. Her followers wanted more paintings, they loved my art and wanted a piece of me in their homes.

We were in shock, so I kept painting, mom would post, and they would go immediately.

After a few weeks of doing this, mom said,

"Kyle, you have something here, people love your paintings, but you our taking over my book page with your artwork. We need to make you, your own page for art."

So, we made a Facebook page called Kyle Brodeur-Artist or @Kyles magical creations.

I started to have followers and it just continued.

Mom started to help me by saying if people are going to purchase these why don't you be fussier and make sure you paint the whole canvas. So that is how mom became my other set of eyes and then we tried out new techniques and it just kept growing to new ideas.

Both of us loved it and it gave us something to do together that we knew nothing at all about.

I enjoy painting with acrylic paints. My mom and I love to paint, it's a two-person effort, she must stretch my arm often. She must always have her hand on my arm, otherwise I tend to raise my arm to my face or up high.

At times it is extremely difficult to paint, it takes a lot of patience and time. Luckily my mother has found easy ways for me to paint by using my hand, fingers, balloons, Q-tips, drains, brushes and now stencils. I love picking out the colors and deciding on what to paint.

I get many of my ideas from Bob Ross and I learn a lot from watching him paint and other artist.

I find a painting that I want to do. Then, my Mom figures out the best way for me to do it. I often use my hands and fingers, then a paintbrush.

If I must draw out something, my mom will do an outline for me with dots to connect. It has worked well for us so far. At times, it takes me a long time to do one painting. I am shocked on how they turn out. Yes, I do make a lot of "Happy Mistakes", but I fix them.

My mother is my other set of eyes and moves the canvas for me and figures ways so I can paint. I could never do this with anyone else cause they don't know the tricks and how my mom and I do everything.

My favorite art is the abstracts, it's the easiest for me, I love picking out lots of colors and seeing how they mix and form all kinds of creations. I am always trying out new drains and techniques. My favorite color for abstract is black, and if I want to make a picture pop, I love yellow.

I do enjoy painting sunsets with beaches and sand. In the winter I love painting trees with snow and cardinals. I tend to use a lot of 3D stickers to make my paintings pop.

When I am not able to paint it is frustrating, my muscle tone can get unbearable, and it could be weeks before I can paint again. When I finally can paint, it is like starting all over again to learn how I did it.

I have to say it gets very frustrating, but it is also so much fun and after my painting is done, I am proud, and in shock that I really did do this.

Mom will put my finished painting on the window so I can look at them from a distance. I look at it and decide if it's complete, do I need to fix something, or if I love it the way it is. Usually, it's something little to fix, and I will have a big smile on my face! My smile tells my mom I Love it!

My biggest worry is my muscle tone is in my neck and at times in my good arm, I must learn to relax and be calm. As I am getting older, and I don't get Botox at Children's Hospital any longer my tone is getting worse. I am trying to get some injections while being awake where before I was put to sleep. We our trying to figure it out and see what I can tolerate.

I hope soon I can get back to painting several times a week. If I can't, I will focus on doing some easy backdrops and my mom will write the inspirational saying on them.

I recently just did a mountain picture with waterfalls; it took me several times to paint it, to be able to finish it. It came out beautiful!

I know I can do some abstracts cause my mom does the tilting with me. I pick out all the colors and drains and I have to say they our gorgeous! At least I will be able to do something containing to art.

The sad thing about a brain injury is you never know when things will change especially with muscle tone. I pray that my good arm will not be taken from me like the rest of my body was.

Last winter I was at a vending event and a woman was looking at my artwork. She asked my mom and I if we ever heard of Chaos and Kindness? We both said, "No".

She told us they selected artist' paintings from people with disabilities and thought they would love my paintings.

If my artwork was selected, they most likely would make a t-shirt out of my design. She suggested that we look into it and submit a painting. Later that week mom looked up Chaos and Kindness, and we decided, to submit some of my artwork and see if they were interested.

I painted a few paintings with sayings and waited to hear back from them. Eventually we heard back from the Chaos and kindness team, and we were asked to do the "Justin live show in the morning". We were excited and we asked Mike DiDonato to join us since we would be running the Boston marathon soon.

Two weeks after we had a great show with Justin Spencer and he learned more about my family's crash and my sport with Mike.

Mom showed him an ocean that I painted, and he loved it. Justin noticed that my thumb is always up and asked me to make a thumbs up painting for them.

I have to say it was extremely hard to do, and whenever my mom would try to video tape me, painting a thumbs up, I would spasm up and couldn't paint. I submitted four thumbs up paintings, and one was chosen with all different colors and my saying, Never Stop Believing in You!

Chaos and Kindness recently launched it with two other designs and now selling a sweatshirt with my design on it.

I just received my hoodie with my design in the mail, and I love it! I am excited that my art was chosen and now have a sweatshirt that was picked from such a great group of people.

They help so many people and making a huge difference in so many lives, especially with people that have disabilities.

Recently I went to their Sky Show in NH. It was an amazing show, with great bands, and the best fireworks I have ever seen. I was so lucky to meet the whole crew from Chaos and Kindness and Recycle Percussion. They really put on an amazing show, and it gave me a night I will never forget!

I loved when Recycle Percussion came on, I have never seen a performance like this, and I loved the beach party. Huge blow-up beach balls so big thrown around in the crowd and we all kept bouncing them in the air.

It was so much fun, and everyone was so happy hitting the ball if it was near them.

They definitely know how to bring smiles to so many people and to have a great time.

I am honored to have a hoodie made from my artwork and to say I met Justin's wife Quinn and Ashley. Yes, I did meet Justin, Ryan and Jimmy and I hope to someday to see them all again.

If I Can Smile, I Can Live

My favorite PCA Dan Healey and me, 2005

Painting an abstract, my favorite, 2021

If I Can Smile, I Can Live

I had the honor to meet
Quinn & Ashley from Chaos & Kindness, 2023

My artwork was selected by Chaos & Kindness and a hoodie was made to purchase, 2023

Chapter Nineteen

The year 2022 has been an extremely hard year for me medically, I have had 4 admissions to hospitals. One for a twisted bowel, one for a new baclofen pump, and two for my Shunt.

My last two admissions were the hardest. I went to the hospital thinking I was having trouble peeing, and just needed a catheter. My stomach hurt it was getting big.

Sad to say after my Cat scan was done, we found out my shunt catheter that emptied in my belly has formed a big cyst of fluid and needed to be drained. I would need surgery to replace my shunt and catheter. The catheter would need to be rerouted either to my heart or lungs to drain.

I was transferred to a bigger hospital that could manage this, I was admitted and after a few days my cyst was drained, and I was told that the chances of my belly getting filled with fluid again was high. My mom spoke to the doctor and said they would touch base next week, and he would schedule a surgery just in case.

A week went by, and my mom noticed my belly was getting bigger again, she measured my belly morning and night to keep track of it.

She called the doctor office to let them know that my belly was filling up with fluid and asked if the surgery date has been set yet?She was told no surgery has been booked.

Mom wasn't happy, she said,

"Can you tell the doctor Kyle's belly is filling up and Kyle will need surgery as soon as possible."

Mom had a zoom call with the doctor later that week and asked,

"Did you scheduled the surgery yet? and he said "No."

"You said at discharge you would book a date and find a team of doctors to help you," he denied he ever said that.

Mom didn't want to argue with him, so she moved on to say we need a date as soon as possible. I have been calling your office stating that Kyle will need surgery and I was hoping you were working on it.

The doctor stated,

"He would schedule a surgery but first he had to find a surgeon to help with the procedure."

Mom was speaking to the doctor's office every day cause my belly was getting huge. Still no date for surgery.

With the weekend approaching mom was trying to keep me home till Monday morning. Mom knew if she took me in nothing would be done medically, and I wouldn't be allowed to drink or eat. It's been around two weeks without eating much and I was losing so much weight already.

Sunday night came I was having severe Gird (Heartburn) I had to go to the hospital, mom called an ambulance. After I was treated, mom asked to have me transferred to where my doctor was. The hospital refused to take me, they said,

"No beds were available." mom then tried to have the doctor that was scheduling the surgery admit me for the transfer, but he denied it.

I was stuck. The hospital I was in didn't want to touch me either, now I'm getting worst from waiting with no medical attention to drain the fluid from my abdomen.

I now have a fever, my white cell count is showing infection, my heart rate is high and now I need oxygen. I had to be admitted to the ICU and transfer hospitals in the same city. We were told my stomach would be drained in the morning. Such a relief we felt to know, I would finally get some medical attention. Morning came and the doctors refused to drain my belly, they worried about infection. Now what do we do?

The doctor that had me said,

"We our trying to find a hospital in the city to take you, that is where I needed to be, it was too serious, and no one here could do this surgery."

Hospital after hospital denied me medical attention, it was crazy. No one wanted me. In the meantime, my belly is huge, I looked eight months pregnant, my gird was still bad but improved some, fever was gone, heart rate was great and thankfully needed very little oxygen. I was stable, but still, we couldn't find a hospital or doctor that would give me medical attention.

After several days the doctor came in and told my mother they were done trying to find a hospital to take me. It was a waste of their time. They had to move on and take care of the more serious patients. Mom was furious,

"What do you mean", she said.

"You're just going to give up on my son?

You our leaving him to die?"

The doctor said "Yes, nothing more we can do".

Mom said, "Did you try out of state?", the doctor replied, "We don't call out of state."

Mom said, "That is not true, our small-town hospital called out of state for us and found a hospital to take my son a few weeks ago."

Doctor replied, "If you find a hospital to take him, I will consider talking to them".

"Consider, mom said?""A hospital won't even talk to us; it has to be a doctor or someone from the hospital to do the transfer."

Mom was furious, telling the doctor,

"How can you do this? He's only 35 years old and deny him the chance to fight to try to stay alive. Kyle has fought for twenty-five years, surgery after surgery and has survived everything against so many odds."

"My son life matters, he may be paralyzed but he lives and is a happy young man. I will discharge him from the hospital." and he said, "It wouldn't be his recommendation and not support us taking him anywhere."

Mom said, "You leave me no choice, if I leave him here, he will die."

Mom went into action, she was crying, and furious. She told me she had to go make some phone calls to figure this out, she told me not to worry.

She called Lenny and my sisters crying. She needed to find a way to save me. She went into the bathroom, and looked into the mirror and said loudly "Mike I need you to give me the answer, tell me how I can help Kyle,

I cant loose him. I will follow my gut just like I always have, please send me the answer." Then mom prayed to God to not let me die without giving me a fighting chance.

The first thing that came to her, was to call my doctors, one of the doctors she called was a doctor that saved my life twenty-five years ago when our crash first happened, Dr. Gerald McGillicuddy.

His office stated to go to the front desk and ask for Dr. McGillicuddy team of doctors that our covering for him. They will come up and evaluate Kyle and get back to Dr. McGillicuddy.

Mom did that immediately, and they came soon after, then they went back to report to Dr. McGillicuddy.

Lenny and my sisters all came to the hospital to be with me while mom was busy trying to find a solution. Mom went on Facebook telling everyone we need to find a doctor and hospital to give me a chance at life, we can't just give up on me.

News spread fast and so many people were praying for me and sharing my mom's video.

A news station came down to do a segment on our story and try to find help to save my life. Mom said she would contact them if she found someone on her own, so they wouldn't have to air the segment in the morning.

Mom and my family were trying to figure out a plan where they could safely take me to another hospital.

We checked into renting an ambulance to bring me to the city, or out of state. We were told they couldn't because it wasn't a discharge. It would be a liability to them.

We thought of trying to put me in my wheelchair and drive a little distance, then call an ambulance. Then thought, they most likely would just take us back to the hospital we were just at and would deny us to go the distance to the big city.

Everything was such a mess, my sister was telling the doctor he could do more, he was choosing not to. In the meantime, I was with Lenny, and I told him,

"My life matters" and Lenny said, "It surely does".

If I Can Smile, I Can Live

"Giving up is not an option for me" I said.

I knew my family was fighting for me, and my mom would find an answer. I was scared, and I wasn't ready to die.

How can doctors just give up on finding me a hospital or step up and give me a chance at life?

I don't understand it. I know I am complicated, but to not even try and save me or drain my belly to give me more time to find a doctor. That is just wrong.

Later that night Dr. McGillicuddy came to my hospital room and said hi to me and looked at my belly and took my family to another room to talk.

He said, "He had a plan",

I was relieved to hear that. Off my family went.

They were gone for a while, I was nervous, but I also knew the doctor had a plan. I knew he cared about me and would do what he could. I thought if he couldn't help me, maybe he would know of some other doctor to help that we could call.

My family came back, it was after 11:00 p. m. My mom told me I would have surgery in the morning to try to drain my belly and try to replace the catheter to a new place in my stomach.

Dr. McGillicuddy will again save your life like he did twenty-five years ago when our crash happened. I was so happy to know I wouldn't die.

Morning approached fast; mom stayed with me. Thankfully I had IV's still in for this surgery. The worst part of any hospital visit is my veins, IVs don't last long and being on three antibiotics, fluids and meds, my veins were all used up.

Mom was allowed in the pre-op room, while I was waiting to be taken into surgery. Mom was talking to Dr. Shaheen Sheikh from anesthesia. She explained the procedure and made sure mom understood and then asked her if she had any questions.

The Doctor was very thorough and then I met Dr. Shakti Nochur. She would help with my stomach to try to drain the cyst of fluid my body formed. She kept me busy talking and keeping me relaxed.

Dr. McGillicuddy came in and said we were set to go, and he would go see my mother when I was finished.

I was so thankful to have my mom with me, she is my security. I told her I loved her, and it brought her to tears. Off I went to surgery.

The surgery took a few hours, I was kept intubated for the night. Dr. McGillicuddy said the shunt was working but he had moved the catheter to another place in my abdomen. Dr. Nochur cleaned out the area of the cyst the best they could and drained some fluid, but the rest would drain on its own.

I was full of cyst, and it would take a while for all the fluid to dissolve. The next few days would be important to see if I would fill back up with fluid. Dr. McGillicuddy said we will have plan B in place if a new shunt would be needed.

I couldn't keep an IV long at all, it became very painful in my arms. I received eight IVs within three days, I was getting anxiety from it. Then no IVs could be placed any longer, I was without one for two days and missing my antibiotics.

I was checked for a picc line but the women had no luck. Later that night a women came in and she said she wanted to look for a vein in my ankle and thankfully she found one.

I stayed in the ICU for a few days then I was transferred to a floor.

I was given a private room because mom stays with me. It wasn't long after, my belly was filling back up, I was then again transferred to a neurology floor. Ultrasound, and the vascular dept was coming in checking my veins for a new shunt placement. Dr. McGillicuddy was getting Plan B in action so he would be prepared on what needed to be done. He named me Mr. Complicated and he knew he had a hard surgery ahead of him.

The next day mom had me up in my wheelchair and I was starting to eat. I started to have severe heart burn; I was put back into bed.

My IVs were no longer working, I had no way to get any meds. The IV Team came to my room, they had no luck getting any veins.

It was a mess, soon after my mom went to check me to see if I needed to be changed and look at my belly. She noticed my pad under me was all wet. She also noticed my stomach was wet from a leaky area, and immediately seen my stomach was draining fluid. Mom left me and said she had to find my nurse.

The nurse placed a bag to collect the fluid my belly was draining, in no time I filled up two bags. I also needed a catheter placed and that attempt was a failure. A doctor had to put in a Coude Catheter that has a curve to be able to pass my enlarged prostate. My heart rate and blood pressure was rising, My heart rate, and blood pressure was rising and I was placed in the ICU, I would need surgery in the morning.

Mom came with me again to the OR, I was worked on for about Forty-five minutes by two IV Anesthesiologist trying to put in an IV line, it was extremely tough, all Dr. Sheikh could find was a little spot near my wrist and thankfully it was enough to put me asleep.

Now the big problem was trying to put in a central line, without this, the surgery couldn't take place. Thankfully after two tries they got the central line in. The Dr. would stay with me during my surgery, just in case if she was needed to place a new line. and now the surgery could begin. The surgery would be a few hours.

To keep mom busy she was making a memory video of our father since it was our twenty-fifth-year anniversary of our crash, in a few days.

It was coming to early afternoon and surgery should have been done by now, mom said she was getting worried that she called Lenny and my sisters, everyone was getting concerned so they all came to the hospital.

Dr. McGillicuddy called to give mom an update and said he was having problems placing the shunt to the heart, he had to call in a team of doctors to assist in finding the best placement. The team decided to put the drainage of the shunt near my lungs. It was their only option. The thoracic surgeon Dr. Karl Uy did the placement of the drainage.

A few hours surgery ended up taking almost 12 hours. It was scary mom said, but she had complete confidence in whatever Dr. McGillicuddy and his team decided to do.

Mom and Lenny could see me after surgery, and I was left intubated so I could rest.

The next day the breathing tube was pulled and now recovery can begin. Mom was told the surgery was a success in placing my new shunt to my lungs.

The doctors did their best to clean out the cyst of fluid and break it up more, to help it drain faster. I also had a huge blood clot and if it wasn't for my filter screen it could have killed me.

The next days were scary I have been filling up with so much fluid and it wouldn't go away. I was told it could be from the blood clot and third spacing fluid that will get better in time, when I start eating again.

Eventually after a few days I left the ICU unit and went to a Neurology floor and after twenty-two days, I will finally be going home.

It will be hard though for mom to take care of me.

I have lots of blood clots in both my legs, I have severe fluid buildup that decreases and increases daily. It could take up to six months to a year for the fluid buildup to go away.

The problem is while I'm in bed I raise my legs above my heart and swelling decreases but as soon as I sit in my wheelchair the swelling starts to back up again. I can't win.

My mom has a lot to figure out with my care and I know it will be extremely hard especially with no PCA's. When Lenny comes home from work then mom would have help.

I am filled with fluid; I am extremely hard to move because I am heavy. When I was on Lasix I could lose nine liters in a twelve-hour period, I was filling up with so much fluid fast.

Hopefully in time my blood thinner will break up my blood clots and make my blood flow easier and then hopefully I won't contain as much fluid.

I have to say I was scared with this visit; I really wasn't sure if I would survive especially when the doctors refused care for me, mom hardly slept the first two weeks, she fought for me, and wouldn't give up. I am thankful to have my mother as my advocate and care giver.

After I went home, I started to lose the fluid so fast, it was a miracle. I was even smaller than I was before. I lost 22 pounds this month from my normal weight of 127 lbs. I was weighed two weeks after I came home only weighing 105 lbs. The heaviest weight in the hospital was 180 lbs. That was a huge amount of fluid I had in my body. My mom thought the scale was wrong, not realizing how much fluid was in my body at that time.

Now I am full of blood clots, and I will be on blood thinner for the rest of my life.

I was discharged to home, but first I went to see Dr. Tanenbaum to fill my baclofen pump then home we went.

It was a busy week getting settled and I had a visit with my primary doctor. I was very fortunate my fluid was all gone within a week, and I was so tiny. I only weighed about 105 lbs. It didn't take long for me to gain some weight back and for my hair to grow in again. Thankfully mom was able to care for me as usual because all the fluid left my body.

I will be forever thankful to Dr. McGillicudy and his team for taking such good care of me, and most of all keeping me alive! I was not ready to die, I still have so much to do here on earth. It's been almost a year now since this nightmare all happened, and I am doing great once again.

I received another miracle! Thank you Jesus, my guardian angel, my father, and everyone who prayed for me to survive! Prayers do work!

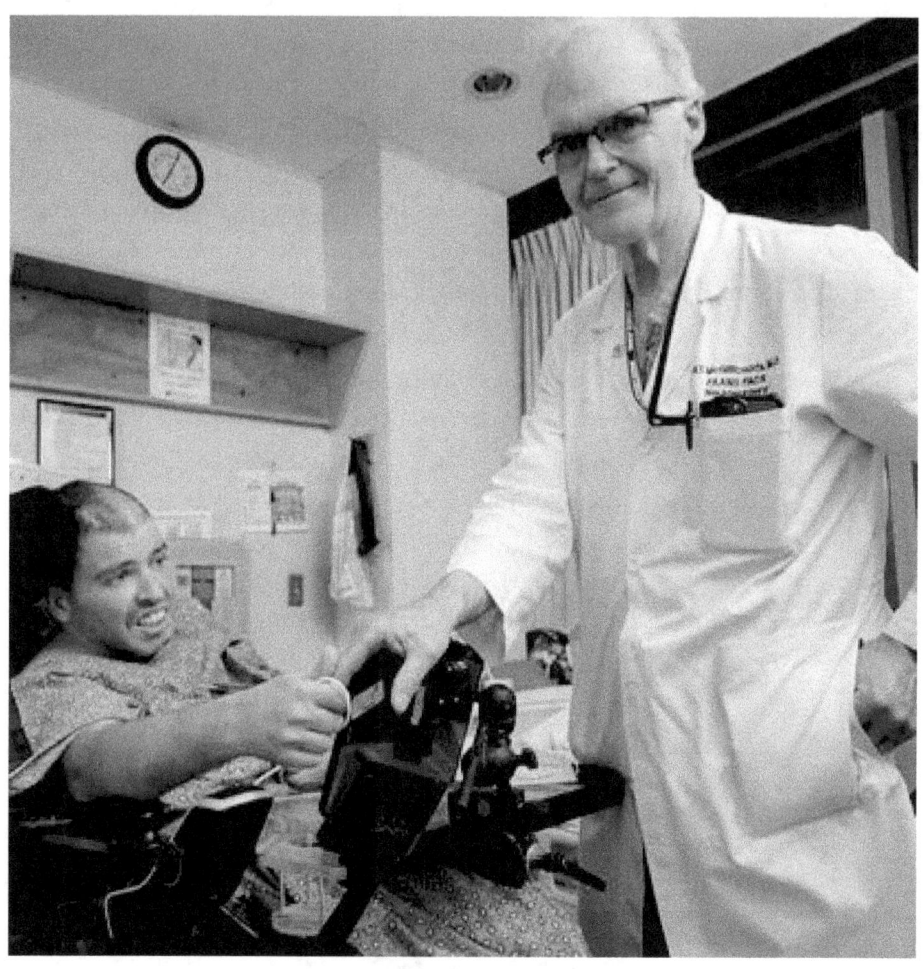

Dr. Gerald McGillicuddy checking on me at 9:00 p.m.
I could never thank him enough for saving my life, 2022

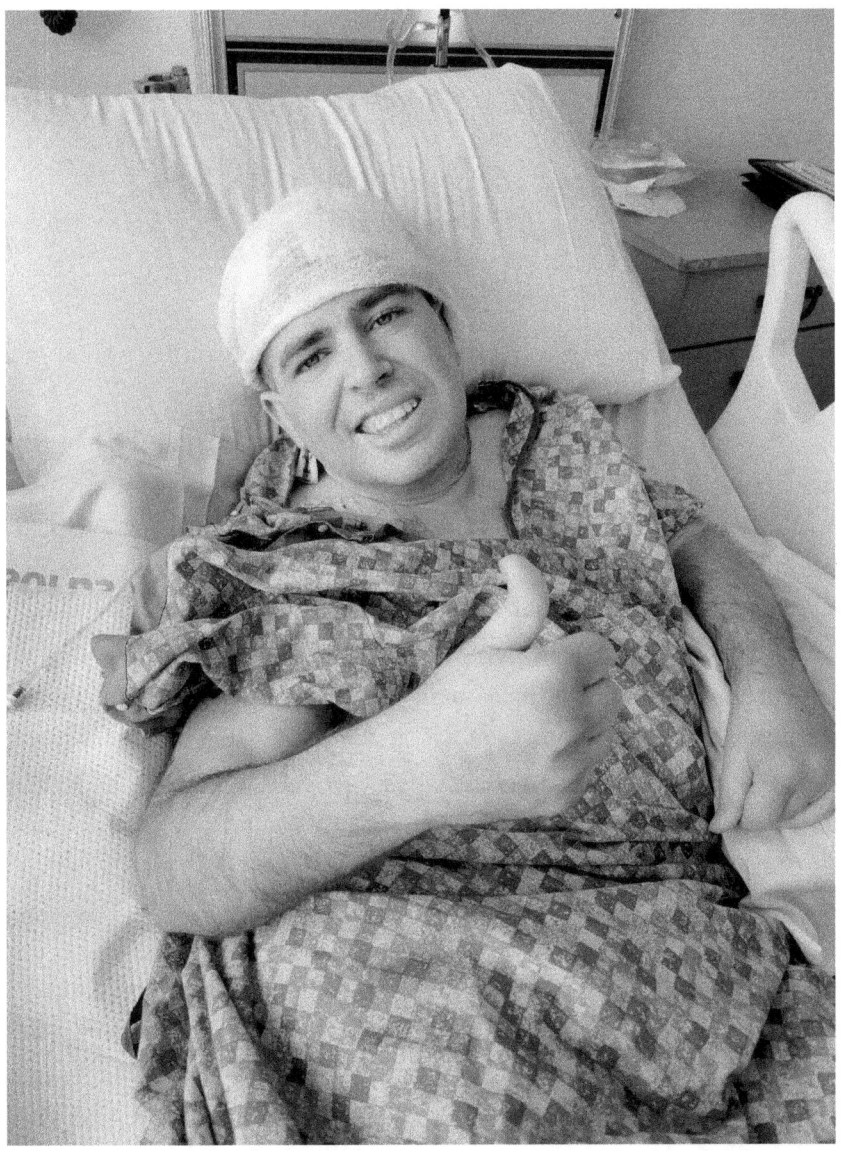

Recovering from my operation of a new shunt placement, 2022

Chapter Twenty

Have you ever met someone that would go out of their way to make you happy without even knowing you?

Well, I have, and his name is Michael DiDonato. We have made so many great memories together with our races that we have competed in.

Mike has brought me so much happiness that would of never happen, if he didn't meet my mom in a bicycle shop in 2011. When Mike suggested he could make me a running chair without even meeting me, mom was shocked!

We have done many 5k & 10k races together and had many great experiences especially meeting so many amazing people. We will forever be grateful to Dick Hoyt and his son Rick Hoyt for starting this sport.

Dick met Mike a year before I had ever met him. Mike gave him a business card just in case he needed help with Rick's running chair. Dick took Mike up on his offer, but ask him, to custom design a new running chair for his son Rick.

Mike and his crew at his father's shop, Southbridge Tool & Manufacturing, designed a new running chair for Rick. Mike had no idea that he would be making another chair for someone like me that he didn't even know.

I will never forget that late afternoon, meeting Michael for the first time at my house. We planned our first race in Sturbridge. I used an adult stroller called the freedom jogger by Advanced Mobility.

It wasn't long after, Mike made me a running chair and brought it over. We were all so excited to try it out, but mom new instantly when she saw it, I would never fit in the chair.

If I Can Smile, I Can Live

My upper body was so curved because I had severe scoliosis and had a spinal fusion. Mike and I were both saddened to know it wouldn't fit me, but Mike said,

"It's okay, I will make another one and it will be wider and longer."

This time around Mike measured me and made sure it would fit me properly.

When Mike and his crew finished the running chair, Mom and I went to his shop to try it out. It fit me perfectly, I loved it, and I was so excited!

Mom was so happy, she had tears in her eyes, knowing I was going to have my dream of having a sport again.

Mike and I took a little run around his shop to see how it felt, soon after we tried running in a race. Since then, I have had many chairs, they just keep getting better and lighter to push. I even have fat Blade tires that can go on rough terrain, and ride on sandy beaches.

Mike and I have met so many great people. The Seven Hills, Chapter of MA Widows Sons, escorted my van to a race in Monson, MA. This was so neat, there were so many motorcycles and many of the riders stayed for the race and cheered Mike and I on.

After doing many 5K and 10K races we decided we wanted to try a triathlon. In order to do that I needed a bike that Mike could push me in. We searched and searched for a bicycle, the prices were crazy, and it looked extremely hard to ride on the handlebars with my body being so curved. As we were looking, and seen the high price tag, we decided to have a fundraiser to help purchase a bicycle.

Mom rented a hall, we had a DJ, caterer, lots of raffles and auction items. People were so generous trying to help in any way they could. We showed a movie of Team Unstoppable, that showed our story from where I was before and after the crash till present.

It was an amazing night with so many people and support for us both. The hall was so full that we had to turn people away. It's a night we will always remember.

As time went on, we had no luck finding a bike that would handle my body and be safe. Mike talked to his co-workers that helped him build the running chairs and they came up with the idea of taking off the front wheel, and make an attachment to go from Mike's Bicycle back tire to the running chair.

It was amazing, and worked great, but more importantly, I would be safe and secure in the running chair and now a bike chair.

Since Mike made my running chair, we kept the money from our fundraising to pay for all our traveling expenses and entry fees to all our races to date. It has been a huge help and it lets us explore so many avenues of races.

Mike and I were excited to sign up for our first Olympic triathlon in Holland, MA. This course was an extremely hilly course. For the swim portion we had to swim ¾ of a mile, I was put in a two-person raft with a rope (tether), attached around Mike's chest to pull me in the water.

When the swimming portion was complete, Mike had to lift me from the raft with no help, and walk over to the road carrying me, and place me in my running chair to do the 25-mile bike ride.

After the bike portion was complete, we had to run six miles. Thankfully I could stay in the chair, but Mike had to take off the wheel extension from the bike and place the front wheel back on, to be able to run with me.

This event I loved, it was exciting watching all the swimmers swim, feeling the wind while riding the bike and being pushed in my running chair. Thankfully it was a nice day for our first triathlon.

During the running part of the race, I wanted to take a water break, so I pointed to it, so Mike would stop. The real reason I wanted to stop was not for water, I hate water, I seen a pretty girl stopping so I wanted to see her. Mike caught on fast, when he seen me looking at her and when she left, I immediately wanted to leave. So, the deal is now, if you want to meet a girl, we will find her after the race, Mike said laughingly!

When Mike and I race we have our language that we use with my hand signs. If my thumb is up, everything is great, if my thumb is down, I need attention. If I use my index finger with my thumb to make a letter C, and I keep bringing my fingers closer together it means a little more to go. I try to motivate Mike to keep going, your almost there. It's my way of helping him to complete the hill we are on.

If I Can Smile, I Can Live

Mike and I have done several triathlons and now we decided we wanted to try a 70. 3 Iron man. This is huge for us. This half iron man consists of 1. 2 miles of swimming, 56 miles for cycling, and 13. 1 miles of running.

We decided to take on the 70. 3 Atlantic City Iron man.

Mike and I were so pumped to do this event. The start of the Iron man was starting, but we were told they wouldn't let me do the water portion because of the wind speed.

The water was too choppy, it would be extremely difficult to pull a boat with me in it. Mike went ahead and did the water portion without me. I was bummed but I knew it was too dangerous to do together.

Mike finished then came back to get his bike and me, off we went, but now the weather has changed it was downpouring! With the roads being so wet and pulling me it made it more dangerous. Mikes back wheel on his bike, had gotten me plastered in mud, I was totally soaked from the downpours. My raingear didn't help me much and I was pooling water in my chair at my waste.

I lost my shades that made it even worse. My body was shaking from being so cold. Mike had to stop a few times to help me, so this delayed our time.

When we finished the Bike race, mom tried to hurry up and get me dry as fast as possible. She didn't want me to continue because I was soaked and cold, she was worried that I could have a seizure.

I wanted to continue, but then we found out we didn't make the time. Mike and I were heartbroken, but we also realized, the weather was not bearable, and it was in my best interest to stop.

For some odd reason Mike and I attract rain at our events. We can handle rain but in an iron man it is so much more dangerous. That night we went to the casino and out to eat and made the best of it, we both agreed, we would be doing another Iron man!

The following year Mike and I signed up to compete in the 70.3 Eagleman Iron Man in Cambridge, Maryland. It figures the weather was rainy and very windy. The swimming portion was cancelled for everyone. The water was too choppy and would be too dangerous for all the swimmers.

Now it was time for the 56 miles in cycling. I was put in my running chair, I had rain gear, glasses, and neck and side pillows on each side of me for comfort. Mike attached the back wheel to the front of my chair, and off we went. We were excited, but the rain was so hard on me again, with the mud hitting my face.

Mike heard me making noises, so he looked back at me, and he seen my hand in front of my face. Mike pulled over, and rotated my body more to the side, so the mud from the back tire wouldn't hit my face so much.

I was stressed, frustrated and discouraged. Mike reminded me we couldn't keep stopping, we won't make our time to continue on.

Mike asked me, "Who are we doing this race for?" I said "Michael David Brodeur".

Mike asked me again "Who are we doing this race for"? I said it even louder "Michael David Brodeur",

Mike said, "That's right! Now let's get this race done! "

The rest of the race I just kept saying my father's name.

When I would see Mike struggle with the hills, I just kept saying Yeah Mike! Yeah Mike!

I knew this gave Mike the energy, motivation and inspiration to persevere!

We arrived from cycling. Mom and Lenny cleaned me up fast, fixed my positioning in the chair, and gave me a yogurt while Mike was putting on his running gear for the 13. 1 mile run.

Off we went, we were excited, we knew after this we would be an Iron Man!

Together we had a great run and I tried to encourage Mike when needed.

The rain calmed down finally, and we knew we were almost done the race.

We could hear all the people cheering us on, we made it, we crossed the finishing line!

We our IRON MEN!

Such a great feeling! I know my father is proud, and he was helping Mike along! We had such a great night, reliving our day and knowing we conquered the rain and hardship.

I am so fortunate to make so many memories. We even got to race on Daytona Beach using my Fat boy tires. We also were thrilled to do a race at Daytona Speedway in Florida. Both races were so exciting.

When we do special races, Mike will stop to take pictures of something special, for example running on the Daytona speedway, Mike put me in front of the American Flag, and took a picture.

We love to try to compete but at times we say, "Hey this is more important we need our pictures for memories". I love how we roll together, and we are Unstoppable!

I am proud to say Mike and I ran the Green River Marathon to qualify for the Boston Marathon in April 2023. This was very exciting for us.

We were selected by Team Hoyt to be the Honoree to run the Boston Marathon. Dick Hoyt and Rick Hoyt, our Legends of the Boston Marathon. This was a huge honor for Team Unstoppable, Mike and me.

Mike had spent a year of getting in shape, he has never run 26. 2 miles ever, before qualifying for the Green River Marathon.

He was on a special diet and would weight train to keep his strength up. A heavy bag was used for kicking and punching.

Mike is not a runner on a normal basis, he will tell you,

"I hate to run, swim, and only bike with his buddies. He will only run with me, during our events."

Mike always says,

"Kyle is the power, heart, and spirit, and I am just the arms and legs."

I find it amazing that he can run like this and never practice for it and especially pushing me in a running chair.

After a year of training for the Boston Marathon, the weekend of the marathon is here. We have an exciting two days ahead of us.

Lenny, mom and I were off to our hotel in Boston. We were meeting Mike There. Soon after we arrived, we went to our room and then went shopping for some memories of the marathon.

That night we had a meal with Team Hoyt it was a great time, with great food and meeting new people. We watched a video from Rick wishing everyone a great run and the message,

"Yes You Can".

Since Rick couldn't be there, they had a cut out of his father Dick and Rick in a running chair. We loved it. We took a group photo, and I had the privilege to meet Zdeno Chara, who was the captain of The Boston Bruins. Chara ran for the Team Hoyt foundation this year. It was a great way to end our night.

I couldn't wait to get to bed and wake up and participate in the Boston Marathon. I was in bed for 9 PM, and was awake at 2 AM, as usual I hardly slept in the hotel, this is why we didn't stay for two nights before the race.

Of course, the weather was not good, it will be a lot of rain, with downpours at times. I did have rain gear to wear, and I was dressed in layers to help keep me as warm as possible.

We were all excited. Mom could take the bus with Mike and me to Hopkinton, Mass, to help get me ready. We were dropped off at a church hall just a few blocks from the starting line.

My morning meds were given to me right before I had to leave. Mike put me in my running chair with all my pillows to help keep me comfortable.

I had my shades to wear, to help with the rain. I was given my flavored water to drink just in case.

Mike was busy stretching, and he ate his granola bar and gummies to help with his muscles. He had some Gatorade Thirst Quencher Powder, to put in his water to drink during the race if needed.

We both were a little nervous and excited we couldn't believe we were participating in this race. I asked Mike to do this years ago, I added it to my bucket list, but Mike knew qualifying under my age bracket would never happen. Here we are and ready to make another dream come true thanks to the Hoyt foundation.

Time to go to the start line, thankfully it wasn't raining hard at that point. Mike pushed me to the start line with all the other people in our division. Now we wait!

My wheelchair was put on a truck to take back near the finish line. Mom had taken a bus back with all the volunteers and waited for my chair to arrive. She then brought my wheelchair to a tent, so it would be there when I finished the race.

The race started, we were off, we started with all the disabled cyclist, and people being pushed like me in a running chair. Mike and I have never been

If I Can Smile, I Can Live

on these roads, every corner and hill were new to us, we just took it all in, as it came.

People were cheering for us all, throughout most of the race, this part was so exciting! At one water station, everyone knew who we were, because they were nurses that worked with my sister, they cheered us on, I loved it.

At one point, a police officer ran with us encouraging Mike to continue and telling him he was doing great!

A friend of ours El Correcaminos, dressed in his Mexican gear ran beside us, cheering us on. It definitely brought smiles to our faces.

Running up each hill were fans on both sides cheering all us runners on. The support was never ending, it followed us to the finish line.

It started to Rain at 10 AM, then downpours started around noon time. Still the fans were there, cheering for us, all day long.

My raingear held up pretty good, but my feet got wet fast and that made me cold. This is only the second time I have ever been in this running chair for this amount of time, I did great even with the downpours, I suffered it out. I was determined just like Mike to finish the race!

Mike was a beast, pushing me along up all the hills and the rain pouring down on his skin and face. Mike was pushing one hundred and fifty pounds for 26. 2 miles, he just kept going, no matter what.

I am sure Dick Hoyt, and my father were using their angel wings, giving Mike the strength to continue, no matter what.

The finish line is coming closer, the crowds our very loud.

Its downpouring, we can see the finish line.

The feeling you have, to know you did this!

You concurred this hard course of 26. 2 miles, in the worst weather, its coming to an end.

Running through the finish line.

Mike slowing down, in tears, his arms in the air, my thumb is up, holding the American flag.

We are both proud and happy that we did this together!

It was an AMAZING time we will never forget!

Channel five WCVB, interviewing us after the race, asking Mike "What this race met to him?"

Mike said, "When I saw Dick's son's, it brought tears to me, I was close to Dick and I know he was watching us, it felt good".

"What does it mean to you to have this moment to have done this and compete this goal?"

Mike said, "It shows a big guy like me, pushing a chair can actually do this, it wasn't a great time, but we finished, and we did it."

"Team Hoyt Moto, "Yes You Can", You can accomplish anything. It goes to show you that if you put your mind to something you can do this."

It is a time in our lives we will never forget. I am so thankful for all the memories that we have made together. I could never have these experiences with anyone else.

Mike is one special man with a heart of gold, not just for me, but for so many others with disabilities.

Mike is changing lives with these Team Hoyt Running Chairs. They our all over the world now bringing happiness to so many people with disabilities.

"Never Stop Dreaming, and Giving Up Is Not an Option" our Team Unstoppable Moto's.

"Yes You Can" Team Hoyt Moto.

Go after your dreams and do it! We only come around this world once, make it happen!

Mike and I finishing our first Ironman, 2019

Mike and I running The Boston Marathon in heavy rain most of the day, we are close to the finish line, 2023

Last Chapter

This year makes 26 years since our crash. Mr. Doucette was released from prison several years ago and released early on good behavior. Keith lives a few miles from our house, and I hope I never run into him. If I do see him, I have lots to tell him, he has no idea how much he has taken from my family and me.

When our crash happened in 1997, I was in a hospital and rehab for ten in a half months before I even came home. Since then, I have had so many sedations and procedures and over 40 hospital stays, and sadly 32 surgeries.

I know surgeries will always be part of my life and will never go away.

But did I have enough?

"Yes, I have".

I still have a baclofen pump, which helps with my severe dystonia. This pump helps to control my spasms by a continuous feed of meds to my spine, then up to my brain. I depend on this to work, just like we need food and water to keep ourselves going. Sadly, when I work myself up the spasms just happen until I can calm myself down.

I have a procedure every thirteen weeks, a needle is inserted in my pump, to drain remaining meds out and refill with new meds.

Every six years or before, I have surgery to replace my pump. In-between the six years I hope I don't get any infections with my catheter that is connected to my spine. We also don't want my pump to mal function in any way.

I have had this pump now for twenty-five years, I have adjusted to it. I look forward to my office visits because I know I will be good for another 13 weeks.

My doctor, Dr. Daniel Tanenbaum, I call him the X-ray doctor. He is amazing on filling my pump; he normally gets the correct spot in his first or two tries.

The doctor uses a guide or at times he just feels around my pump on my lower right side of my stomach. This pump is the size of a hockey puck. The problem is you can't see through my skin, so it is difficult to do at times, especially if you have a lot of scar tissue.

The Dr. is feeling for the area where he will insert a needle. Once he finds the correct place then he will drain the remaining baclofen in my pump, and then put the new meds in.

I know I am a difficult patient, but he is the kind of doctor that likes the challenge and he is happy to be able to help me out. I hope he keeps me forever; I love his personality and he is very good to me.

As I get older my body keeps changing. I never use to get cold, now I do. I am finding winter is getting harder for me to handle. My muscle tone is spreading more in my neck and now in my good arm.

We our working on this, and I am hoping medicine will help.

A lot of my bad habits that I formed during Covid our pretty much gone now.

Every day in the morning I would grab onto my bed bars so tight, and I would turn purple at times. This was scary for my mom; she would always tell me to breathe!

My right arm is still impulsive, especially when painting, and I am left alone to do it. I need my mother's hand on my arm, it helps to keep my hand where it should be.

For example, using my I-pad, I can't just type a sentence like you do, it takes me several minutes. I tend to move my hand upwards to my face, my impulsivity kicks in. I always hold something in my right hand, it does help some. Otherwise I am grabbing my shirt to try to type.

If my mom is holding my arm, I do much better, but she can't do this for me all day long. My I-Pad has always brought on Impulsivity for many years, some years our worse than others. Presently I don't use my I-Pad as much because I don't want to stress. Hopefully in time I can use it more often again.

I formed a habit of talking while I was eating, and it often got me in trouble. Everyone was worried that I would choke. My mom even purchased three De-Chocker's just in case a few years back. I have one in the kitchen, in my backpack and one in my bedroom.

Early in 2023, I choked on a piece of chicken. I was turning purple, my mom hurried up and grabbed the De-Chocker and placed it around my mouth, pumped it twice, and the piece of chicken was released. If I didn't have that De-Choker handy, I could have died.

Mom said,

"Kyle, I don't know what's going on here, but you could have died in the hospital if I didn't find you a doctor a few months ago and now this. It seems like someone is trying to take you from me, but they aren't getting pass your mama! "

I just looked at her and smiled with my thumbs up!

Thankfully I have improved in not talking so much while eating, my mom started giving me food pouches and it seemed to help stop me from talking.

I formed a very bad habit of hitting myself in my head. I was having anxiety of the thought of new PCA's starting or if I knew I was going to be doing something I was excited to do.

This was extremely hard for mom to see. She had to walk out of my room at times, because she had a hard time watching me do it. She got to a point where she just ignored it while helping me, she would have me put my hand behind my head. I have to say this did help and I don't do this as much anymore.

My muscle tone will be a problem for life. I have more problems now since Children's Hospital will no longer allow me to be a patient because of my age.

I was able to be sedated for many years for the Botox injections. Dr. Donna Nimec was very good to me, and I miss having her and seeing all the pretty nurses at Children's Hospital.

Dr. Tanenbaum is trying to do some injections to me while I am awake. I had my session of only six needles, I did okay, but I don't think I could do thirty or more in one sitting. My good arm is tight at times, and it is affecting me with everything I do.

Mom is trying so hard to loosen my arm. I started taking extra medicine in the mornings, it is helping some. I do know half my problem is me, I get myself to excited and I tense up.

I have another bad habit now of my right hand always on my face, this isn't good because I am squishing my cheek and causes me to bite it.

Mom is worried that I could cause open sores in my mouth and cause infections.

I tried an elbow brace, but it didn't work, my tone kept moving it and I got out of it. I was given a hand brace for my hand, but I used my mouth to get the straps off. Mom can't win with me. I feel like when she put a contraption on me it made me worse.

Hopefully in time my brain will change again, and I will stop this bad habit on my own.

With extra medicine and breaks before supper time, it does help me out to relax more. Laying on my back helps a lot, I still prefer my side, but I know I can't any longer.

I am never told any more if someone is coming over or if I am going somewhere. Now I am told things at the last minute, so I don't get so excited. At times I will find out when we arrive at places to play it safe. I have to say this has worked to keep me calmer.

I only can wear one shoe, on my left foot. My right foot is so turned and bent that I don't fit in a shoe or sneaker. Yes, I have tried foot braces, after having foot surgery. It did help my left foot, but my muscle tone took over my right foot curving it once again. The brace couldn't help because my tone was too severe.

So, what's my favorite brand sneaker? I love Jordan Sneakers, I have over 14 pairs. Yes, I have the right foot sneaker in my closet, we keep saying we need to donate them to someone that may have just one right leg to use.

It's hard at times with everyone always putting drinks and food in front of me. Drink this and eat this, sometimes I don't like it or I'm not in the mood for it, but I have no choice because that's what's for supper and I need to drink.

Breakfast, it's my choice I get whatever I want. I tend to like Cinnamon sticks during the week and on weekends, my mom's homemade pancakes.

At least my mother doesn't make me eat food I dislike; she tends to make what I can eat and will enjoy. I need soft food and meat needs to be cut very tiny. I tend to get takeout or eat out at least once or twice a week.

I am very bad with eating; you need a lot of patience with me. Sometimes I can take an hour just to consume a little meal. I admit, I am lazy and the only time I will eat fast is when I am hungry and want what is in front of me. Overall, I eat well, I love my mom's cooking and baking. I love junk food, and she always makes sure I have something that I love.

I do need a guardian, who is my mother to help advocate for me, make medical & financial decisions, and to handle everyday task. I need help with everything I do in life. Thank God for my family for the great care they give me. PCAs are hard to find, it seems like no one wants these kind of jobs any longer.

I do have a seizure disorder, my seizures are not the normal seizure, I do not show the symptoms like the average person would. I am always a puzzle, my brain is severely damaged and like my neurologist said years ago, whatever I do is a miracle, and it's amazing that I am not in a vegetation state coma.

Do I get frustrated and sick of people taking care of me?

Of course, I do, I want to be like everyone else and do things for myself. At times it's hard for my PCA's or family to help me, you must have a lot of patience. Especially when I am tight and if I am holding your hand and I can't let go. It's always been a problem for me. I know caring for people like me or anyone with a disability and health issues, caregivers do get burned out. It's a hard job caring for someone else and dealing with a brain injury can be stressful. I would give anything not to have these diagnoses and have a normal brain and life.

Being paralyzed and dependent on every need is very hard for me, at times I do get upset and feel angry.

At times I would ask my mother,

"Why is my life so hard"? Her response was.

Kyle, we will never know why this happened to you and why you were chosen to live like this, but people that can talk, walk, eat and live that so called, "normal life" that you want, have a lot of trouble dealing with life also.

It's not all happiness, they must go to work every day, support a family, and find their way through life with their own personal struggles. Some people have severe addictions to drugs, alcohol, and some have depression, or other illness where family couldn't be of help to them. Some don't want the help, or find it too hard to stop their struggle through life.

Life can be extremely difficult for many. Some believe their life won't get better and they don't know how to escape it, they feel trapped. It is very difficult to find the strength and courage to move on, and get the help they need so that life can get better. Sadly, some choose to take their own life. Loss of a loved one is extremely difficult. Grieving for a loved one is different for everyone and it's very hard to continue life without them.

Some people look at you and say how come you're so happy, when your life is so hard?

It goes both ways, and all I know is that you are AMAZING, you were left here to help me, and your sisters to survive this tragedy. You are helping others to make better choices and decisions while driving, and you are an inspiration to many people to handle their own life journey. Your father is so proud of you and for keeping his memory alive".

I know my mom is correct, and she always finds a way to help me deal with my losses and a different way of looking at life. I must focus on all the good I have, but at times it is very hard.

I don't think I will ever get over the want to walk again or to have my own family. I want so bad to have a girlfriend and get engaged. I would love to be able to go purchase a beautiful diamond ring and have a big wedding just like my sister's and friends had.

I have never been kissed, a real kiss from a real girlfriend. I want what everyone else wants, I want to be loved by my person, my soul mate, my best friend.

I am not shy, I do try with the girls, but I don't get anywhere, the girls are always so polite, hold my hand and kiss my cheek. I am thankful but I want more.

One day I asked mom, "Do you miss the old Kyle?"

She said "Yes of course I miss the old Kyle, but I love the new Kyle just as much and I wouldn't change a thing about you"

"You are still my favorite son, and you bring me so much joy and happiness. I am blessed to have you."

I said, "I am so different now, I can't walk or do anything for myself."

Mom didn't care. She said,

"She loved me no matter what", and guess what, she really does. She is by my side every day, and I can't get anything pass her. Sometimes this is tough though.

Overall, I am a happy go lucky guy, I learned to make the best of it. I do have a great life considering my disabilities, thankfully I am rich in Love from my family and friends.

A brain injury is real, our brain changes often and produces behaviors we have no control over. We form habits that will come and go, but one thing I have learned is that the body just gets worse with age. We must be thankful for what we can do and look at the good in our life to survive it all.

I am glad I lived past ten years old, and I can't believe I just turned Thirty-six. I am not sure what the future holds for me but whatever it is, I will never give up and hope for the best.

July 13, 2023, was the date my grandmother Rita Brodeur passed away at the age of 103 ½ years young. This grandmother of mine was very special to me, she was my father's mother.

I met her when I was one in a half, mom and dad were only dating at the time. Mom said when we met her, she asked Rita what I should call her? She told me to call her memea. So memea it was. I would love to go visit her; she always gave me ice-cream in a cone. I would love to pretend I was Batman and jump off her table then Uncle Ronald or dad would catch me. Dad would also pretend to be the joker. It made it so fun for me.

Memea loved to hold me in her rocking chair and singing me nursery rhymes, and some she would make up of her own, especially when she did the piggies with my toes.

I was lucky enough to live next to her at the young age of three, mom and dad took the apartment next to her since it became available, and they would soon be getting married.

Growing up next to her was the best, she was always so concerned if I was hungry or if I wanted a snack. I loved how she would always keep potato chips, gumdrops, Werther's hard candy or mini chocolate bars with other candy on her table. There was always something good to eat.

She would watch me outside while I was on my rollerblades, skateboard and bicycle and I made her nervous. She would get nervous because I would go fast and do jumps, she always was afraid I would hurt myself. Often, she would go back inside her house.

As I got older, I realized I called her memea but she wasn't my blood grandmother. Even when my adoption went through and I was a Brodeur legally, it still made no difference in how she treated me. I was her grandson from the day she met me.

I realized as I got older what a gem of a person she was, she loved me unconditionally, just like my father did. My grandmother went to all my school events, she never missed anything, and she showed me love all the time.

Sadly, when our crash happened, she lost her son, my father Michael. She was so heartbroken, but her strength and faith in God carried her through her hard days and sadness. Mom always said, she not only helped with us kids but helped her to be the best mother she could be.

My grandmother even gave up her home so mom could build an addition to her apartment. Mom hated to ask her, but she had no choice, she wanted me home with her. No one wanted me in a nursing home and be several hours away.

Memea didn't hesitate, she said whatever I need to do, I will do it. She didn't want me in a nursing home, she wanted me home where I belonged. She always felt so bad for me and prayed for me every night.

Not many people would do what she did for me. She stayed and lived in her apartment through all the construction, she sacrificed so much, and never ever complained.

I always loved to see her and when we moved from our apartment and built a house in Charlton, Mass, it was a huge adjustment for us all. We would go visit her often. We mostly visited her in the summer, and we would sit outside. Getting me into her apartment was hard because of my wheelchair.

Memea would come to our home often with Uncle Ronald and Aunt Pit. We all stayed very close. When I had surgeries all three of them would come to Boston Children's Hospital to visit mom and me.

My grandmother never had a license to drive, she depended on her family to take her places as needed. It all worked out though because we had so much family that lived next to each other. Everyone always helped each other as much as needed.

My memea worked part time in a factory right next door to us. She finally retired when she was 82 years old. She always was full of energy and cooked for all the holidays. We were lucky just to be next door and not have to go out in the cold. She never liked much help, she liked to do everything herself. She would always tell people to go sit down and she will do it later. But of course, no one would listen to her.

As I got older every time she would see me, she would give me a $20 bill. She did this for years, mom would always tell her he doesn't need any money and she would argue back and say if I want to give him a little something, I can. Mom always lost!

I of course had a smile on my face. Memea would always say to my mother "The poor kid, he goes through so much, enough is enough", "I pray for him every night to be out of pain". Each time she seen me she would kiss my forehead and when I or her had to leave she would say "Okay, Love you, See you later."

Her favorite saying was "It Is What It is" and isn't that the truth. I painted her a painting with that saying and she was happy. She always wanted to hear about my events weather it was painting, my sport or spreading awareness. She was proud of me and loved how I kept my father alive, and she said how proud he must be of me.

I will never forget her, and I will always be thankful for the love she gave me every single day.

In the last two years, my grandmother started to decline more every day. I didn't get to see her as much, but I loved her. When I did get to see her, I would always make her something with pops. I made her a heart on Valentine's Day, then for her 100th birthday in December I made her a Christmas tree made with 100 pops, she loved it. She would eat two pops at once.

I had the sweetest, kindest, loving grandmother ever! When she passed, I was very sad, but happy for her that her struggles of everyday life were over. I will hold her in my heart, right next to my father.

Three weeks after I lost my grandmother, I lost my grandfather Eugene Matte on 8/7/23. My pepea was 86 years old. He would come visit almost every week. My grandfather raised canaries in his younger days, and he was a Master Canary Breeder and had many "Best in Show" Champions. He specialized in the "Gloster Canary".

When I was little, he would take me in his bird room and show me the birds. He would take a bird out of the cage and let me pet it. Then I would go chase the rabbits in his backyard. Since my grandfather was a barber, he gave me my first haircut. All my little baby curls were cut off, and now I had a big boys haircut.

When our crash happened, my grandfather took it very hard, he came to Boston often to visit me.

He would love to tell jokes and could whistle loud like a bird. He knew several whistles of different birds; he was really good at it.

My grandfather never learned how to read or write but he was a smart man considering how he taught himself how to be a carpenter, woodcarvings, and carve birds. He loved to care for his yard, he had the greenest grass around and beautiful flower trees.

He would love to do a magic trick with a quarter and make it disappear and call himself Dr. Fedue or Dr. Fedell, this was always funny, and he loved to dance.

Several years ago, pepea came to visit and he was sitting on the couch, and he asked mom where I was? Mom yelled to me to come in the living room, I came rolling down the hallway.

Mom had no idea I had my new water gun on my tray. I stopped, aimed my water gun at my grandfather and I shot the water right between his two eyes.

He jumped so high; I scared the living daylights out of him.

We all were laughing; I was lucky he wasn't mad at me. I was belly laughing and so wasn't my grandfather. I have to say this is one of my best memories of him.

The last several years my grandfather had Alzheimer's, it was very hard watching him decline and become a different person. Thankfully my father's wife Fay, took great care of him. Fay new him well and new how to manage him when he had his episodes.

As the time went on, my pepea became quieter, no more jokes and he didn't say as much. I am thankful he never forgot me and would always say Hi and bye to me. I didn't like to see him like that, I would always tell mom it's so sad.

When my grandfather passed, I felt bad, but I also knew it was for the best. Now he is at peace and with his family in heaven. I know when it's my turn to pass, he will be waiting for me. R. I. P. Pepea, I love you!

Now the weeks, months and years ahead our healing times for our family. I just hope and pray we don't lose anyone else.

Mom said we need to adjust our life once again, without these two special people in our lives. We will miss them, but when we remember them, they will bring smiles to our face.

She knows they would want us to continue living the best we can, and they will be looking down at us with pride.

I want to leave you with the special message of loss.

On the days you feel fragile and broken,

Know your strength and courage is making you beautiful, in ways you may not see now.

Hang in there, keep moving forward and know it will be all right.

One day you will look back and see how the broken pieces came together and created something wonderful, inspiring and uniquely you.

If your hardship is through loss, your loved one will be looking down at you, loving you more than ever, knowing you chose to still live.

After all, Life is for the Living, and life must go on no matter what our losses are.

I am excited to have my book, and hope it will inspire others to continue living your best life possible. It doesn't matter if you have a disability or not, we all have real genuine feelings, and wants in our life. After all, we are all human. I will continue to make the best of this life and always remember,

If you can SMILE, you can LIVE! - Christopher Reeve.

My grandfather Eugene Matte and me, 1998

If I Can Smile, I Can Live

Kyle, Kimberly and Katie with their grandmother Rita Brodeur

Printed in the USA
CPSIA information can be obtained
at www.ICGtesting.com
LVHW010344150624
783213LV00012B/485